CHRISTMAS BARITONE UKULELE
FINGERSTYLE | CHORD MELODY

UKELIKETHEPROS
© 2024 TERRY CARTER

ISBN-13: **9781958192177**
UKELIKETHEPROS.COM
© 2024 TERRY CARTER

TABLE OF CONTENTS

Christmas Baritone Fingerstyle Chord Melody	01
Amazing Grace - Level 1	03
Amazing Grace - Level 2	05
Silver Bells	07
We Three Kings - Level 1	11
We Three Kings - Level 2	13
Silent Night	15
O Come O Come Immanuel - Level 1	18
O Come O Come Immanuel - Level 2	22
The First Noel	25
Deck The Halls	27
Jingle Bells	29
Santa Claus Is Coming To Town (BONUS)	32
Great Job!	33
The Essentials	A
How To Read Tab	B
Notes On The Baritone Ukulele Neck	C
Baritone Ukulele Hands	D
Baritone Ukulele Parts	E
Understanding Chord Diagrams	F
Chord Chart	G
Music Symbols To Know	I
About The Publisher	K
About Uke Like The Pros	L
About Terry Carter Music Store	M

CHRISTMAS BARITONE UKULELE
FINGERSTYLE | CHORD MELODY

The holidays are a time like no other—a season filled with joy, warmth, and cherished traditions. There's something about Christmas that stirs our hearts, bringing families together, lighting up faces with smiles, and filling the air with music that touches the soul. Now, imagine being the one to create that magic, playing timeless holiday songs on your baritone ukulele. With this Christmas Baritone Ukulele Fingerstyle Chord Melody Book, you can turn your baritone ukulele into the heart of your holiday celebrations.

There's a reason the baritone ukulele has become one of the most beloved instruments in the world. Its soothing, resonant tones have a way of lifting spirits and spreading happiness. Add the wonder of Christmas to the mix, and you have the perfect recipe for a holiday season filled with unforgettable moments. Whether you're gathered around the Christmas tree, entertaining guests at a festive party, or simply playing for yourself, the baritone ukulele brings a sense of intimacy and charm that no other instrument can match.

This book is designed to take your baritone ukulele playing to new heights, introducing you to the beautiful world of fingerstyle chord melody. Unlike strumming chords alone, chord melody weaves together the melody and harmony into a single, seamless performance, making it sound as though you're playing with an entire orchestra. It's a technique that allows you to fully express the joy and warmth of the season with just your baritone ukulele.

The songs in this book were carefully chosen to capture the essence of Christmas. Classics like Silent Night and Deck the Halls will bring nostalgia to everyone who hears them, while joyful tunes like Jingle Bells and Santa Claus is Coming to Town are guaranteed to fill the room with laughter and cheer. For a touch of elegance, you'll find beautiful arrangements of Amazing Grace and O Come O Come Immanuel, with options for simpler or more advanced versions, so you can choose the level of challenge that suits you best. And of course, pieces like The First Noel and Silver Bells add the perfect finishing touch to your holiday repertoire.

But this book isn't just about the songs—it's about giving you the tools and confidence to make these pieces your own. You'll find detailed, step-by-step instructions for each song, breaking down every melody line, chord transition, and lyrics. As a free bonus, we've included downloadable backing tracks at both slow and fast tempos.

The holidays are a time for creating memories, and there's no better way to do that than with music. Picture your family and friends gathered around, listening to the sound of your baritone ukulele as you play We Three Kings or The First Noel. Imagine the smiles and laughter as you launch into a lively rendition of Jingle Bells, or the quiet moments of reflection as you strum Silent Night. These are the moments that make the holidays truly special, and this book is your guide to bringing them to life.

The baritone ukulele has the power to transform any occasion into something magical, and Christmas is no exception. With the Baritone Ukulele Christmas Fingerstyle Chord Melody Book, you'll have the chance to create music that not only delights but also connects. It's a way to share the spirit of the season with those you love and to create memories that will last a lifetime.

Don't let this holiday season pass by without experiencing the joy of playing these beloved Christmas classics on your baritone ukulele. Dive into the Baritone Ukulele Christmas Fingerstyle Chord Melody Book today, and start creating the soundtrack to your most magical Christmas yet! Let's make this holiday season unforgettable—one beautiful note at a time.

To Play Fingerstyle With This Book:

The easiest approach to playing fingerstyle for this course is to use your thumb to play notes on the 4th string, your index finger to play notes on the 3rd string, your middle finger to play notes on the 2nd string, and your ring finger to play notes on the 1st string. This method ensures smooth, natural movements and helps you master the beautiful arrangements in no time.

Now is the perfect moment to put this technique into action and start learning enchanting new Christmas songs on your baritone ukulele. With just a little practice, you'll be wowing your friends and family, transforming gatherings with the warmth and joy of timeless holiday melodies. Imagine the delight on their faces as they hear you bring these classics to life with a style and confidence that will leave a lasting impression.

Don't wait—unlock this incredible talent today and let your baritone ukulele be the star of this Christmas season!

FREE BACKING TRACKS

Amazing Grace
Level 1

This song is in 3/4 time, meaning 3 beats per measure and the quarter note get the beat. The song is in the key of D Major and the melody starts with a pickup note on beat 3. It's important to only play the strings indicated by the melody in the notation and the TAB and to follow the fingerings in the chord diagrams.

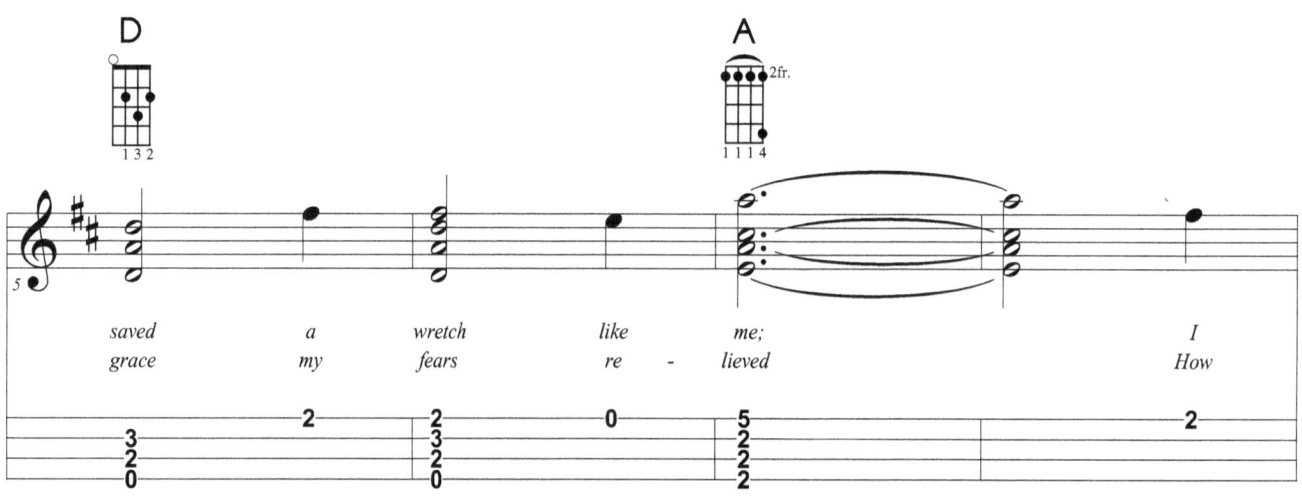

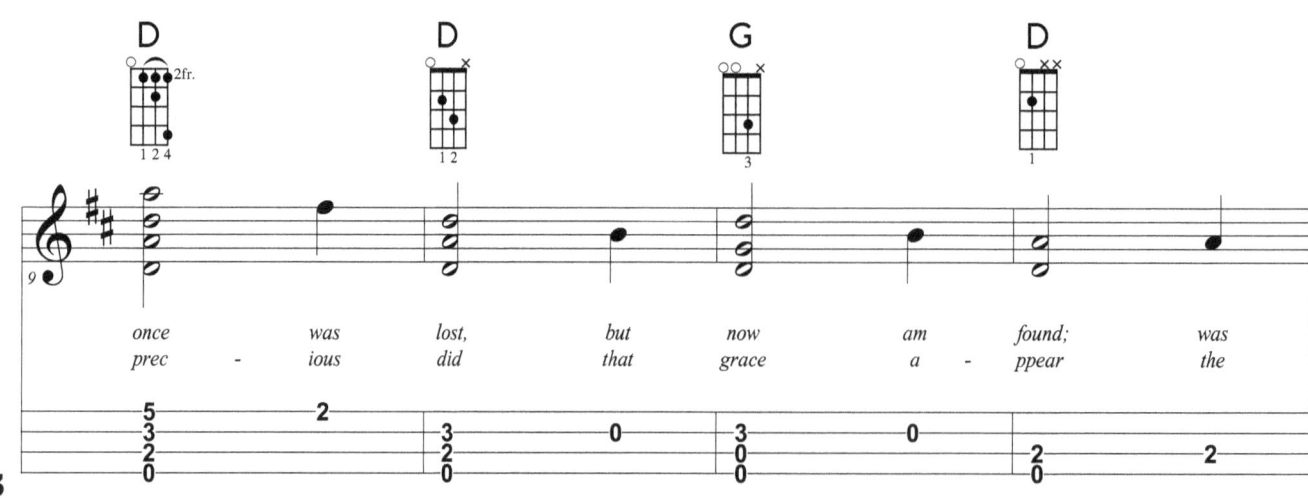

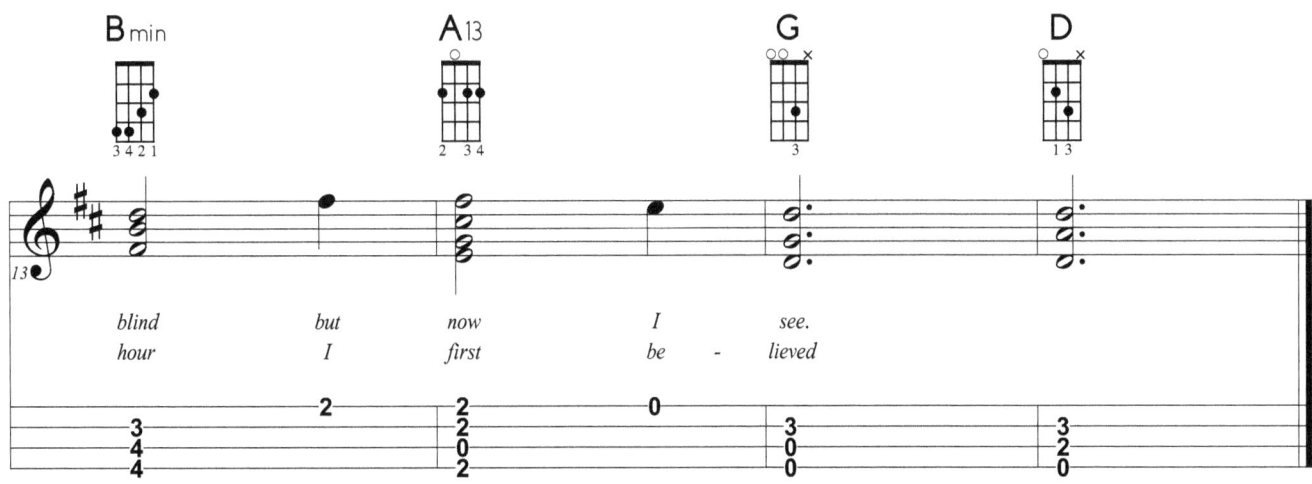

The Story Behind
AMAZING GRACE

"Amazing Grace" is one of the most beloved hymns in the world, often sung during the holiday season as a reminder of grace, hope, and redemption. Written in 1772 by John Newton, a former slave trader turned Anglican clergyman, the song carries a powerful story of transformation. Newton penned the lyrics as a reflection of his own life—a man who was once deeply lost but found redemption through faith. His experience during a perilous sea voyage in 1748, where he survived against the odds, marked a turning point in his spiritual journey. It was this moment of realization that inspired Newton to write about the boundless grace he felt saved him.

The hymn's cultural significance is immense, transcending religious settings to become an anthem of hope and resilience in times of struggle. "Amazing Grace" has been embraced by numerous communities and movements throughout history.

It was famously sung during the American Civil Rights Movement in the 1960s, becoming a song of solidarity, strength, and a cry for justice. It has also been performed at countless memorials, offering comfort to those mourning and reminding them of the power of grace in times of sorrow.

One lesser-known fact about "Amazing Grace" is that it originally had no melody of its own. The words were sung to various tunes until the early 19th century, when it was paired with the melody known as "New Britain"—the version we know today. The song's universal appeal is also reflected in the sheer number of recordings it has inspired; it is estimated that there are over 7,000 recorded versions of "Amazing Grace" across genres, from gospel and folk to rock and even jazz. Artists like Aretha Franklin, Elvis Presley, and Judy Collins have all offered their unique interpretations, helping to solidify its place as a timeless piece of music history.

"Amazing Grace" continues to resonate today because of its simple yet profound message. It reminds us that no matter how lost we feel, there is always a path to redemption. Its enduring popularity speaks to our shared desire for hope and the belief that, even in the darkest of times, grace can lead us home.

Amazing Grace
Level 2

Page 1 of 2

This Level 2 version is identical to Level 1 except for the addition of a triplet in measures 1, 5, and 13.
A triplet is when you have 3 notes per beat and since the triplet happens on beat 3 it is counted 3-trip-let.
The first two notes of the triplet are a pull off from the 2nd fret to the open 1st string.

John Newton
Arr. Terry Carter

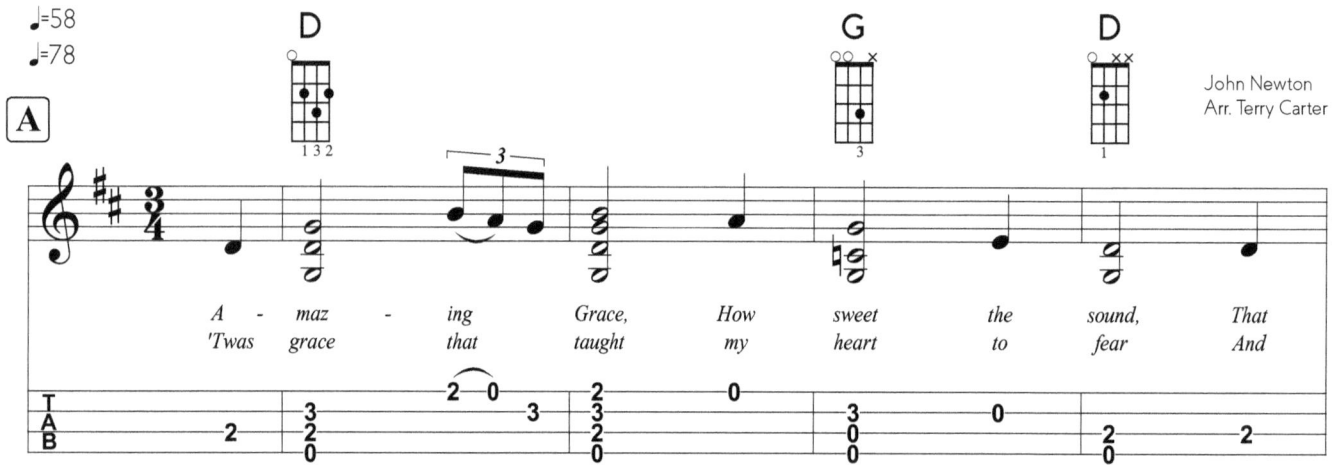

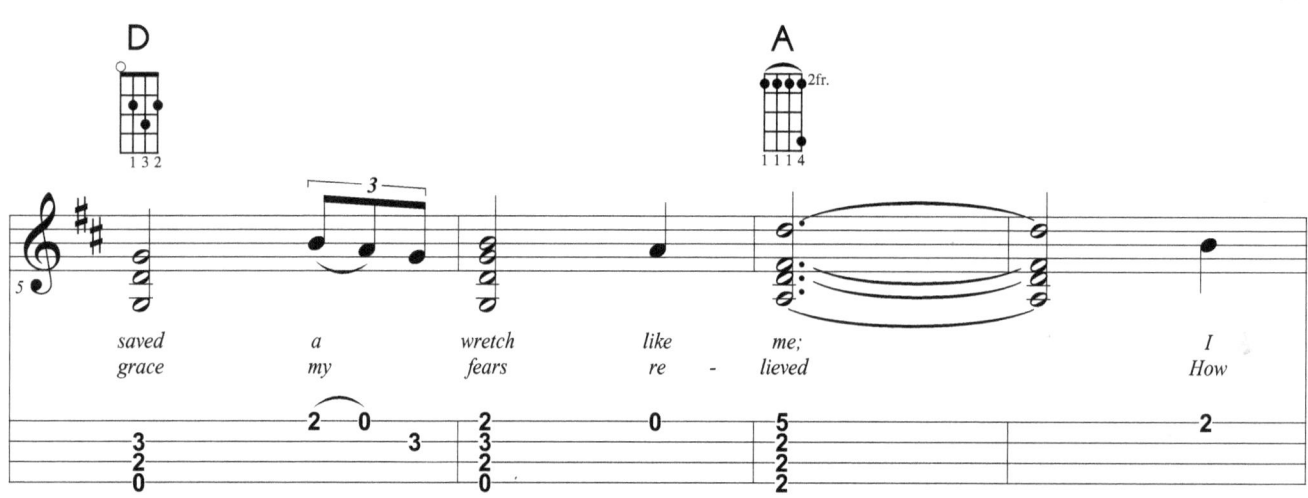

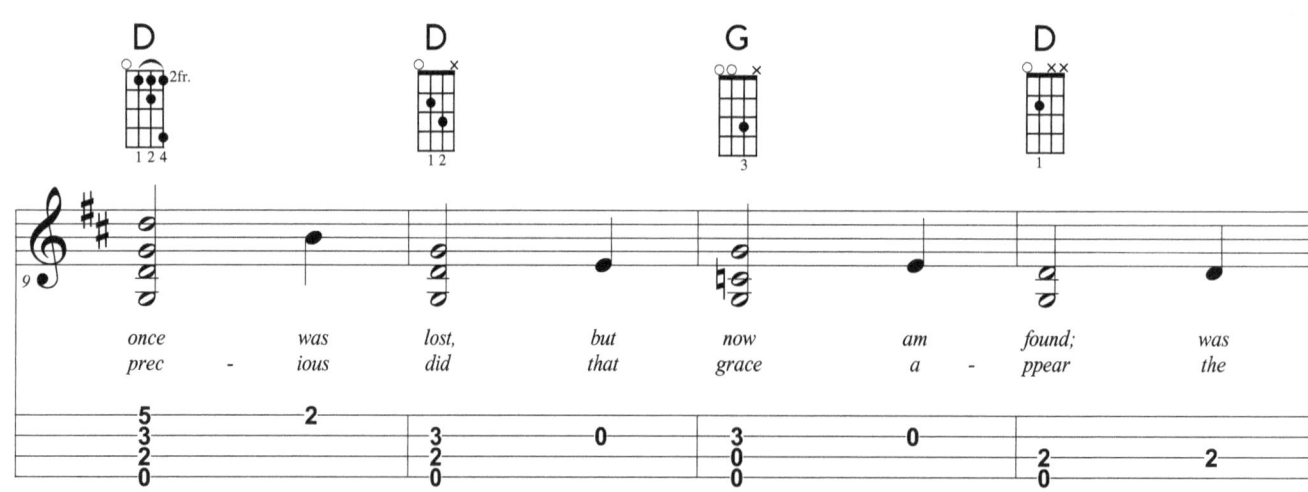

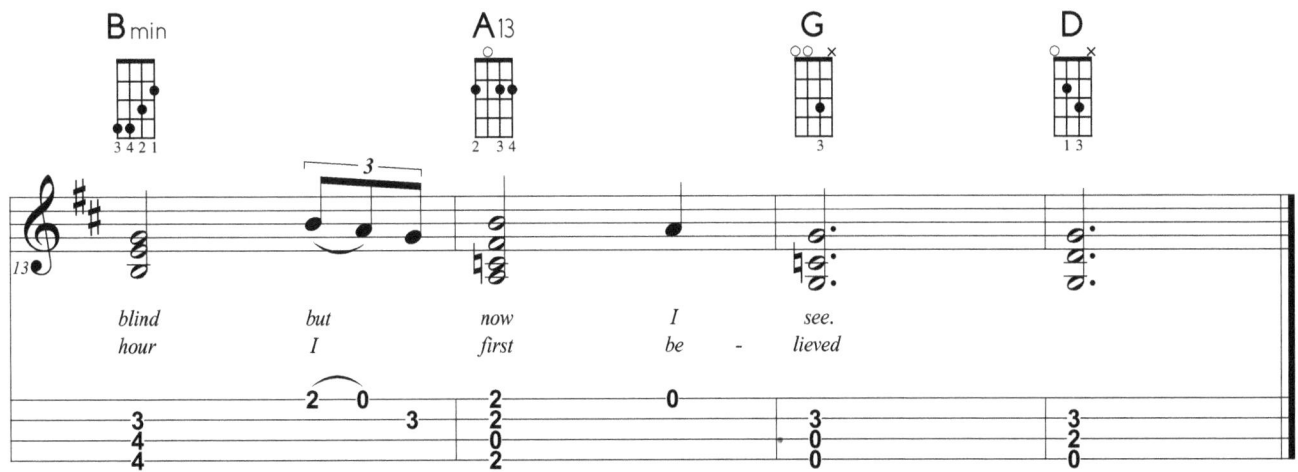

UKE LIKE THE PROS
PLATINUM MEMBERSHIP

INCLUDES:
- Access To Over 40 Courses
- Early Access To All New Courses
- FREE Weekly Practice Sessions
- All Beginner, Intermediate, And Advanced Courses
- For Ukulele, Baritone And Guitarlele
- Access To Workshops
- Access To Challenges And Giveaways
- ULTP Song Catalog
- Special Discount For ULTP Merch
- Downloadable Backing Tracks
- Downloadable Tab And Music Sheets
- Access To ULTP Community
- Access To ULTP Forum
- Access To ULTP Members Guide
- 30 Day 100% Money Back Guarantee

UKELIKETHEPROS.COM/PLATINUM

Silver Bells

Page 1 of 4

This song is in the key of D Major, in 3/4 time, and starts with a pickup of eighth notes on beat 3. The melody for this arrangement covers all 4 strings and uses some great chord shapes like the opening D chord, the Gmaj7, and the chromatic A, Ab, to G progression.

Jay Livingston
Ray Evans
Arr. Terry Carter

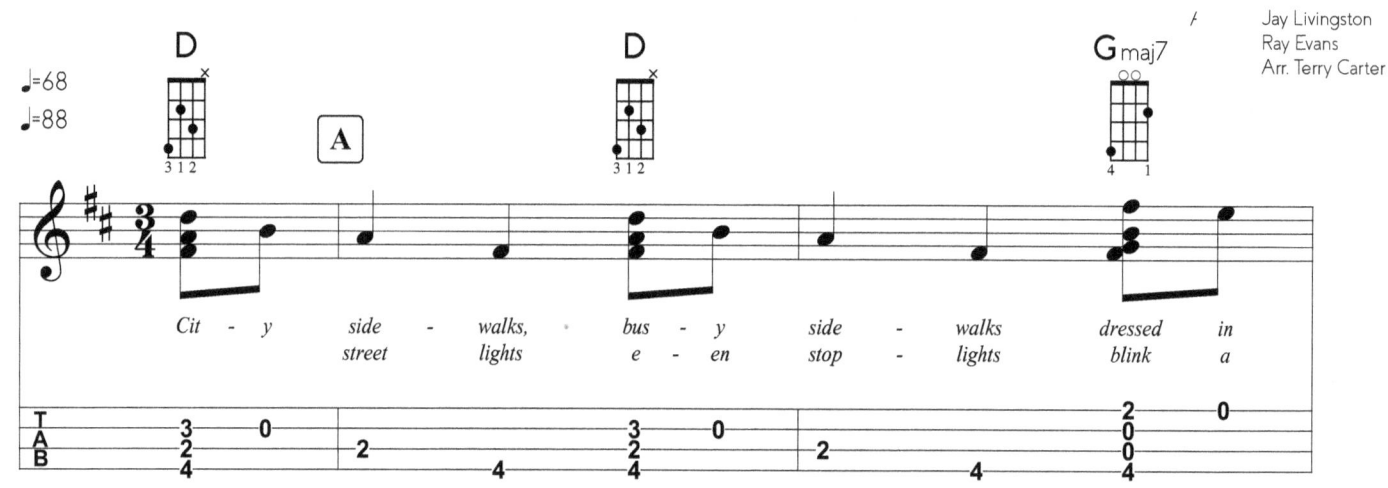

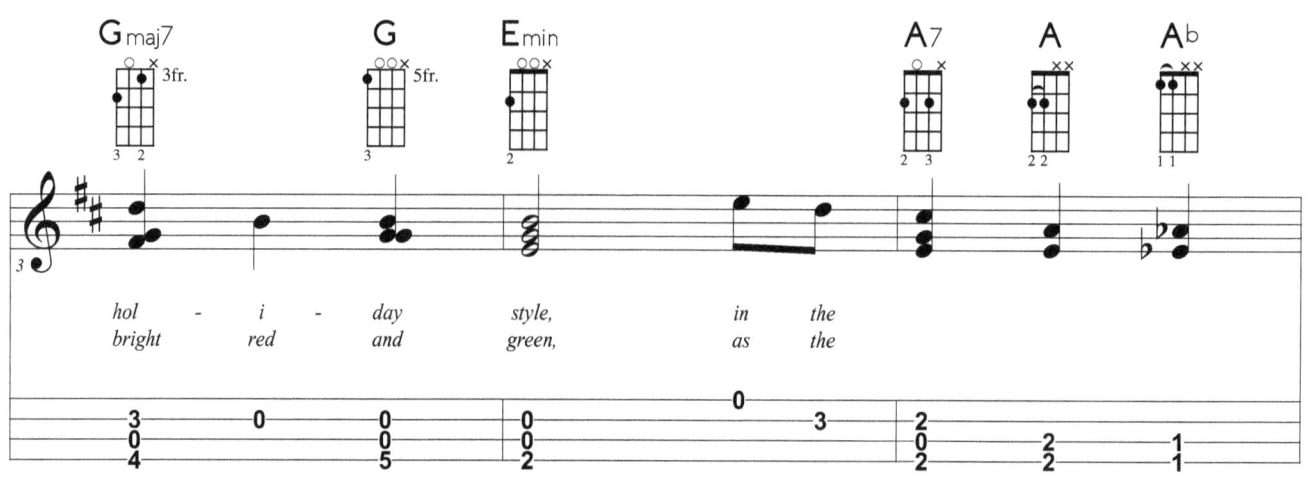

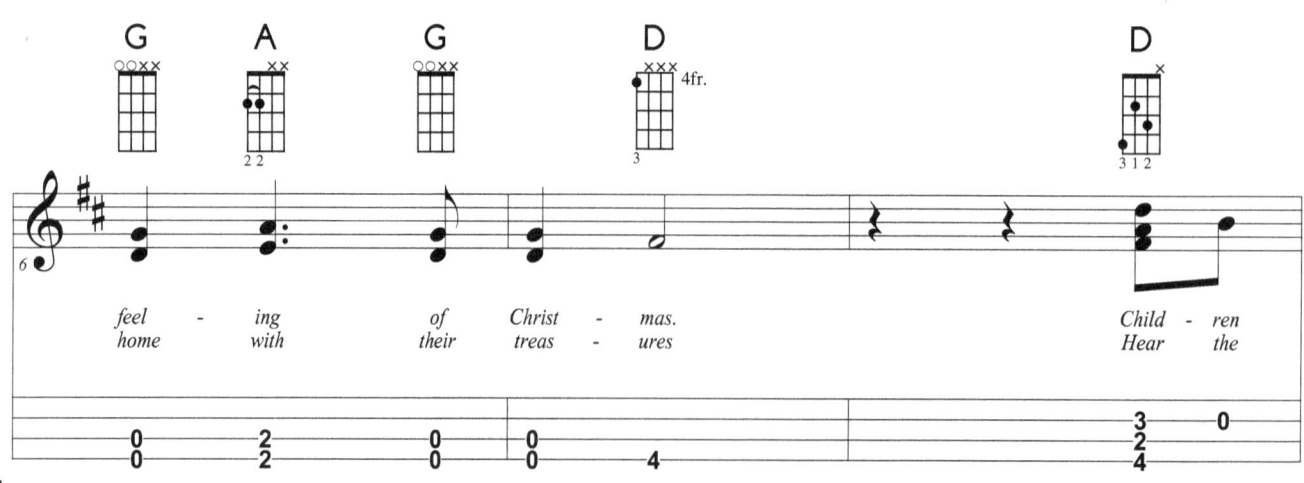

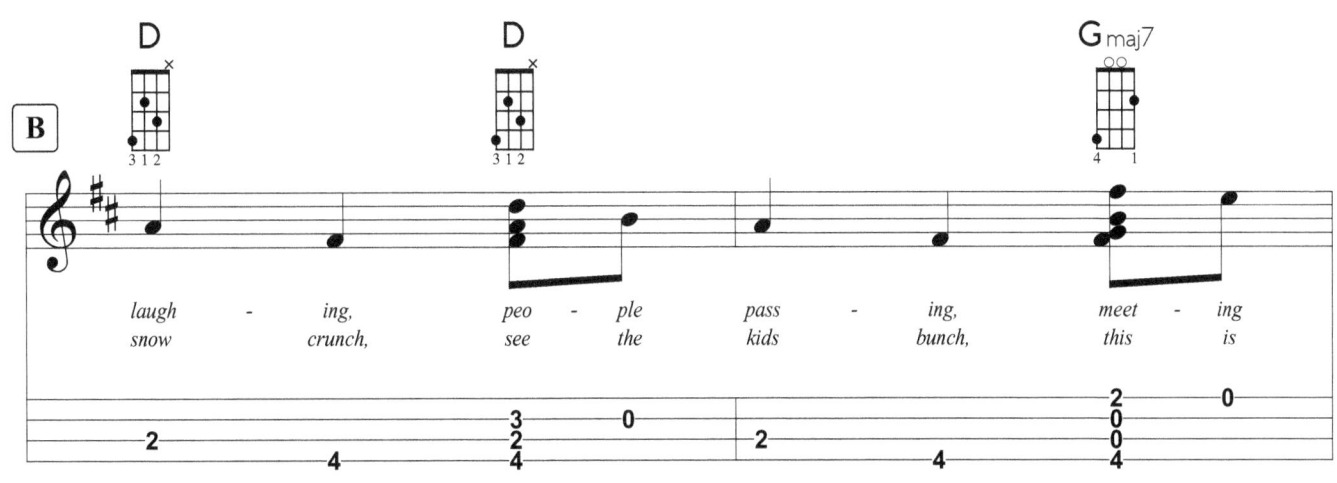
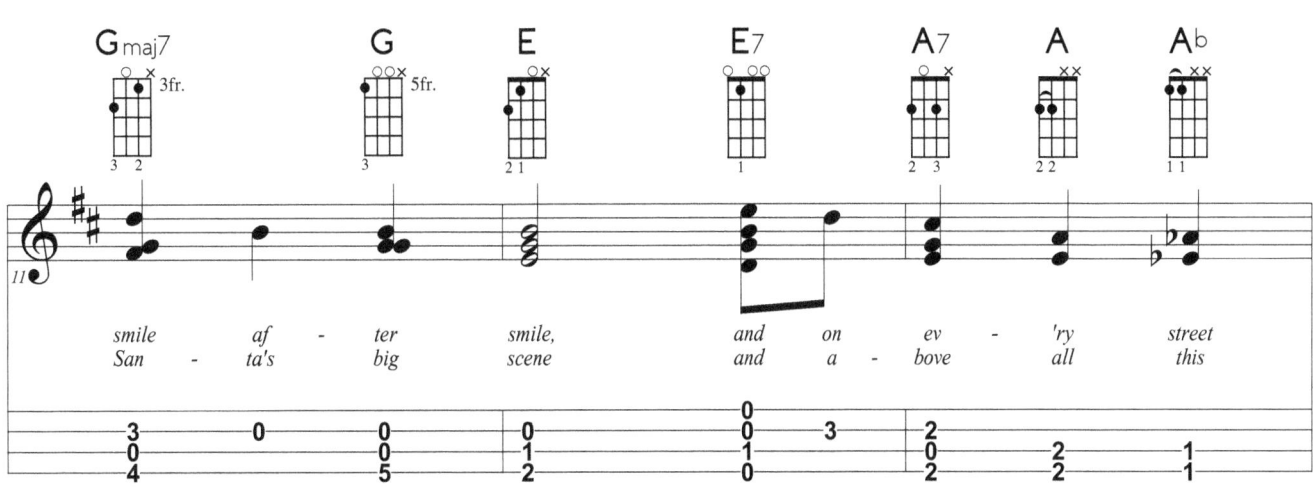
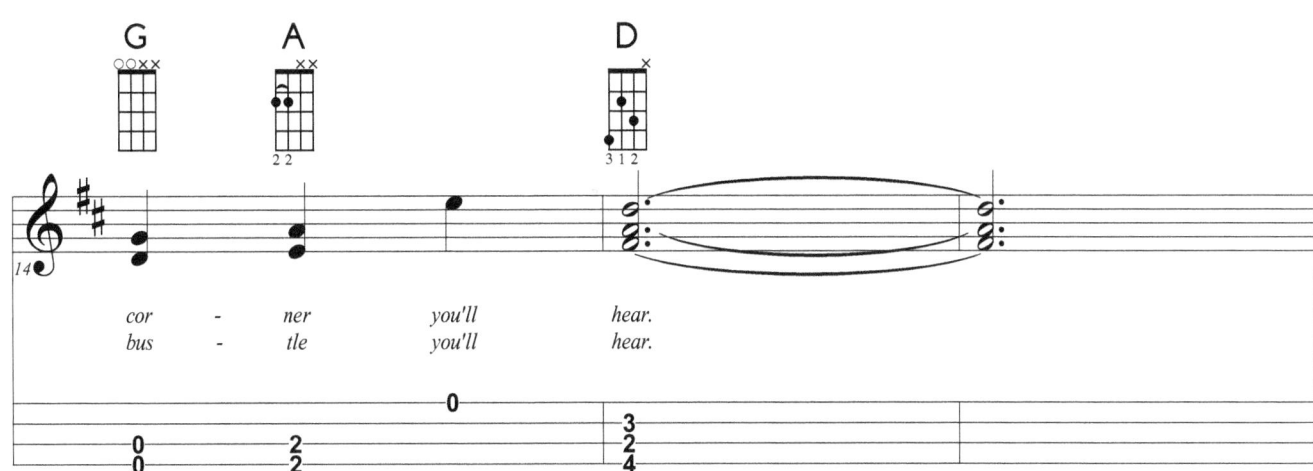

Silver Bells

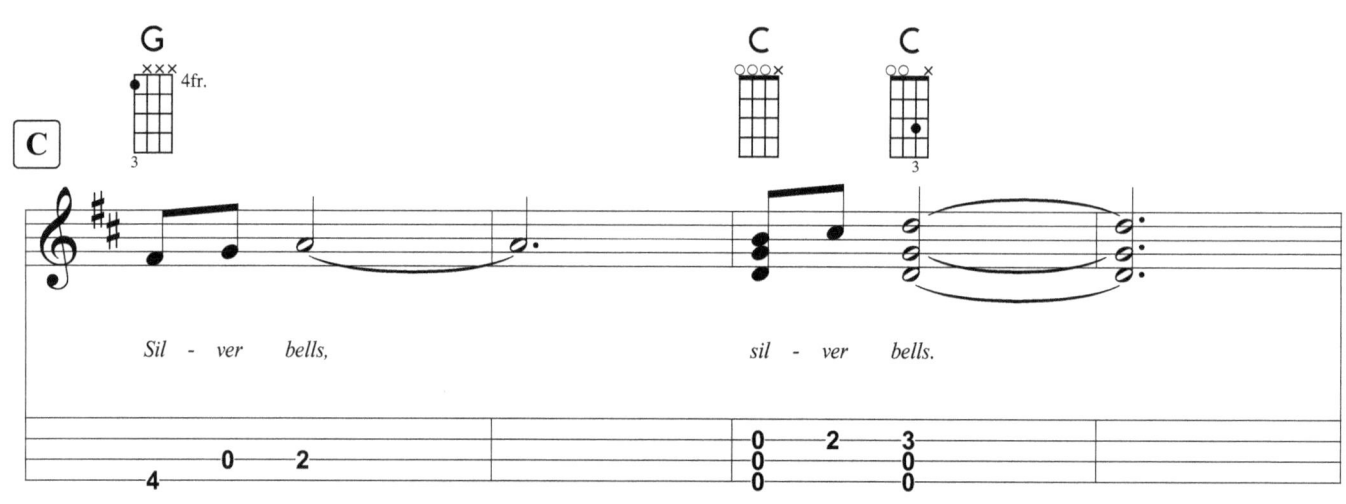

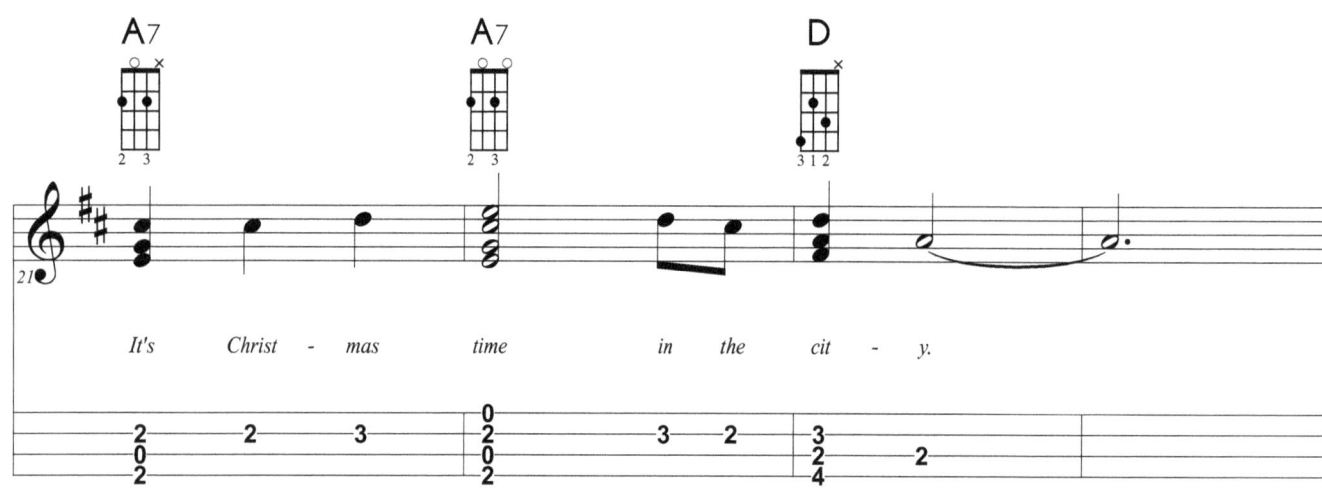

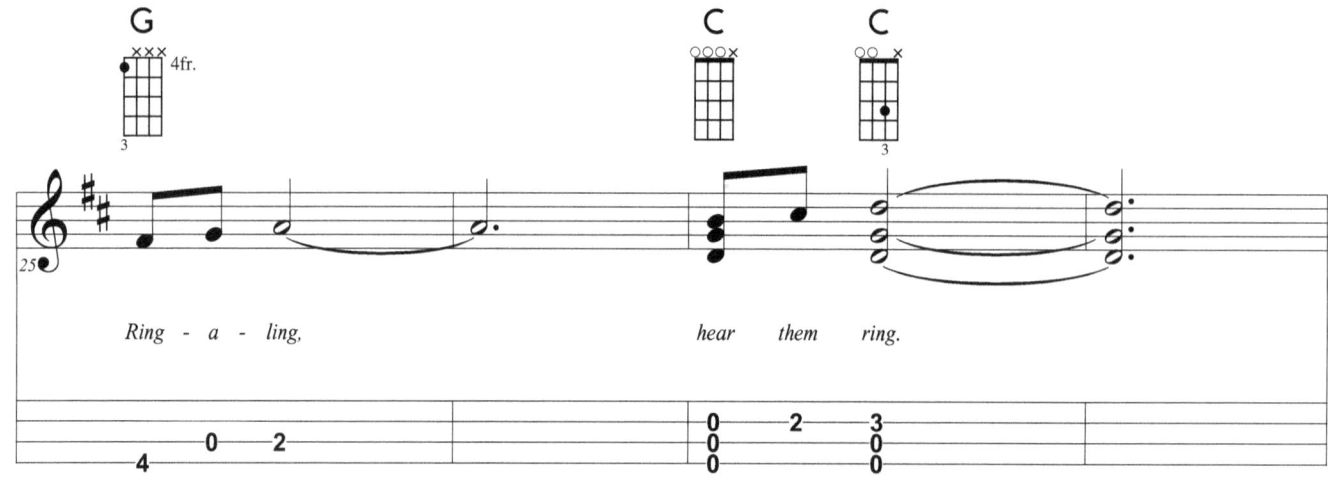

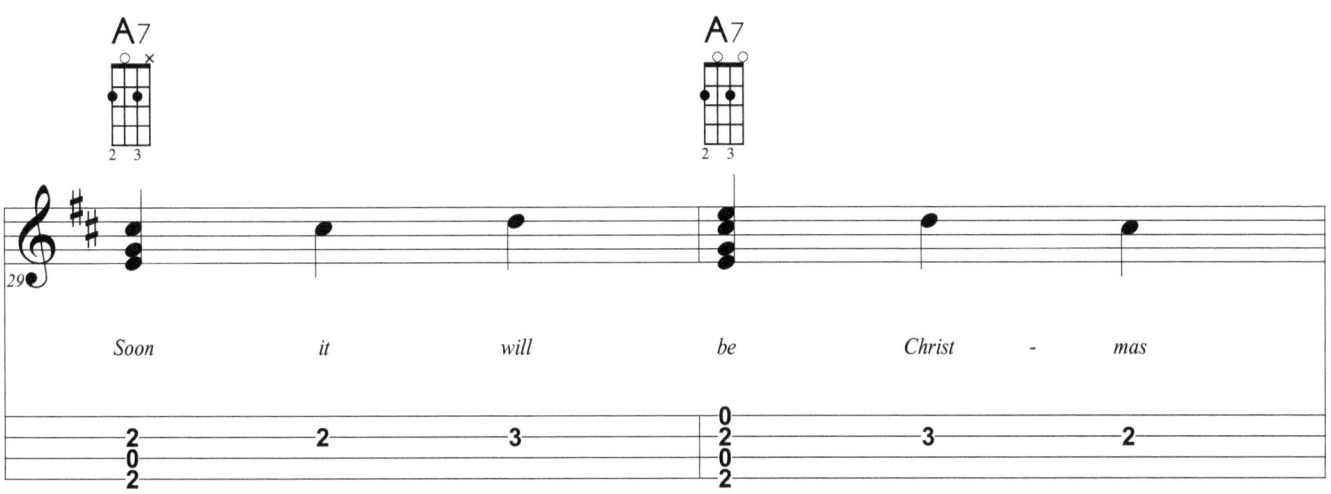
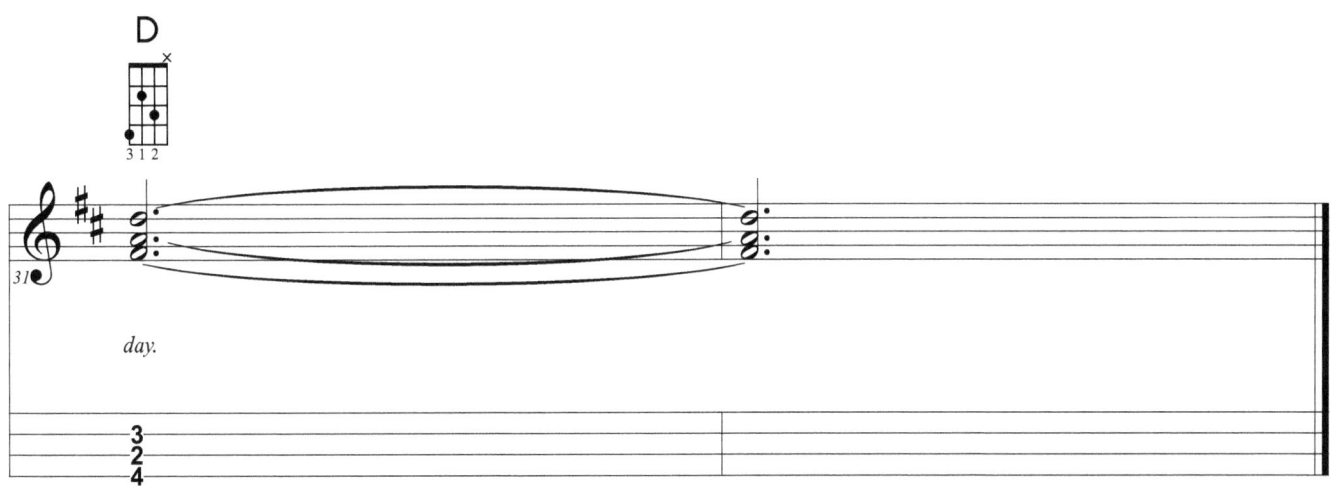

The Story Behind
SILVER BELLS

"Silver Bells" is a classic Christmas song that has become synonymous with the festive season. Written by Jay Livingston and Ray Evans in 1950, the song was inspired by the sounds of Christmas in New York City, particularly the ringing of Salvation Army bells. Originally titled "Tinkle Bells," the name was changed after Livingston's wife pointed out the unintended connotation. The new title, "Silver Bells," captured the holiday magic they aimed for. The song's first major performance was by Bob Hope and Marilyn Maxwell in the 1951 film The Lemon Drop Kid, quickly gaining popularity. The melody evokes a nostalgic sense of the holidays, painting a picture of bustling city streets filled with shoppers, bright decorations, and the familiar ringing of bells. "Silver Bells" has been recorded by countless artists, including Bing Crosby, Perry Como, Dean Martin, and Michael Bublé, further solidifying its status as a holiday standard. Each rendition has kept the song fresh for new generations of listeners.

"Silver Bells" almost didn't become a holiday classic, as Livingston and Evans were initially uncertain about its reception. However, its depiction of the festive urban landscape resonated deeply with listeners, and it soon became a staple of holiday music. The song endures as a holiday favorite because of its evocative lyrics and joyful melody, capturing the magic of the season. It reminds us of the simple joys of Christmas—shopping for gifts, hearing bells ring, and seeing bright lights that transform cities into winter wonderlands. Its timeless charm makes it a song that brings people together, evoking cherished memories and the true spirit of the holidays.

We Three Kings
Level 1

Page 1 of 2

This song is in the key of A Minor giving it a darker more somber tone. There aren't a lot of chords in this arrangement so its important to focus on bringing the melody to life. A few of the highlights are the moving melody notes for the E7 chord and the C chord.

John Hopkins Jr.
Arr. Terry Carter

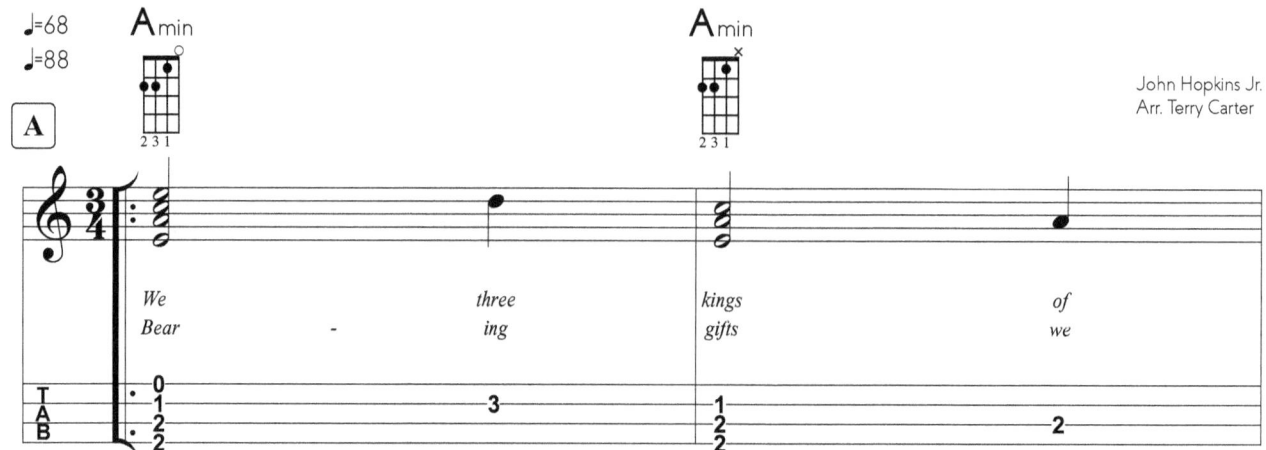

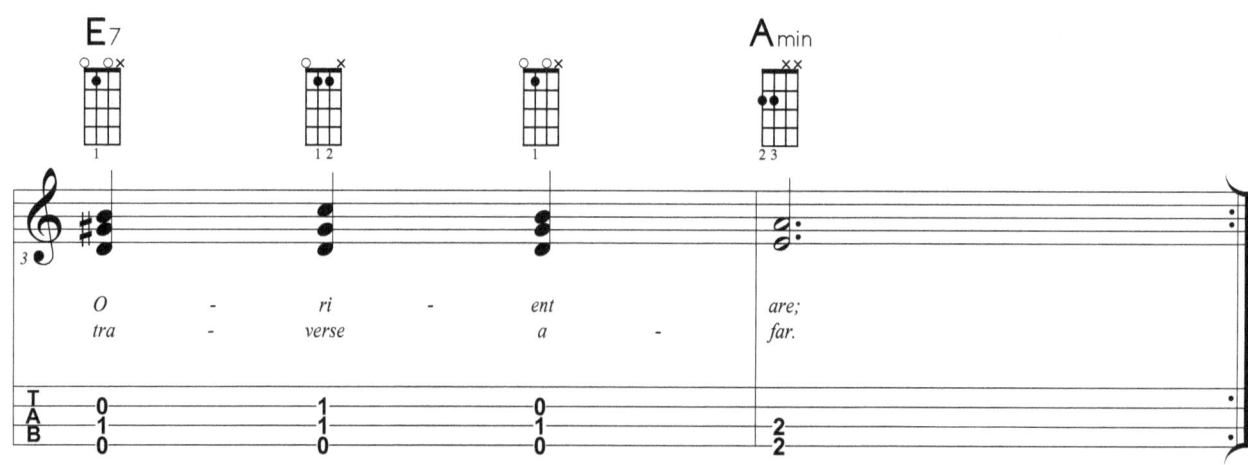

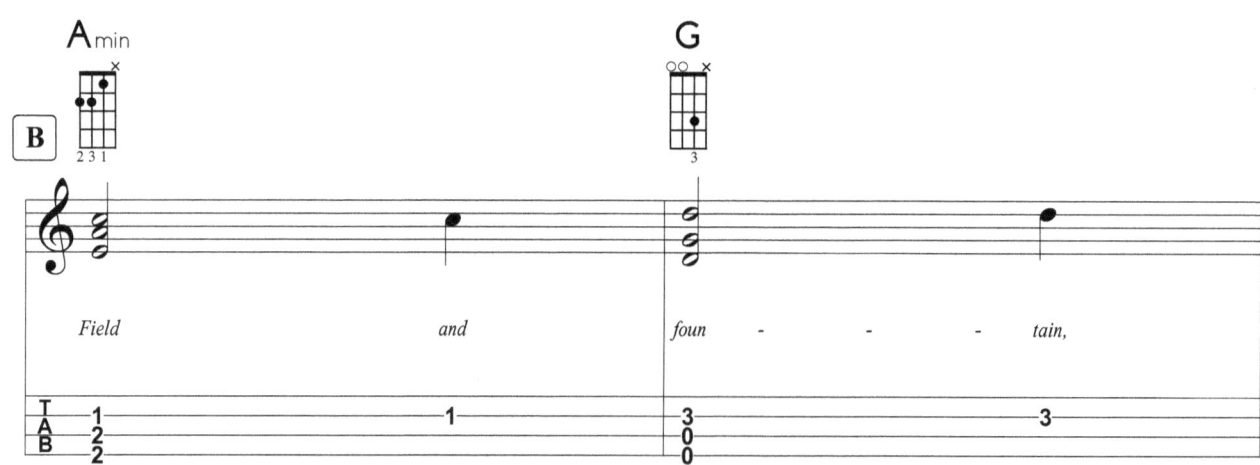

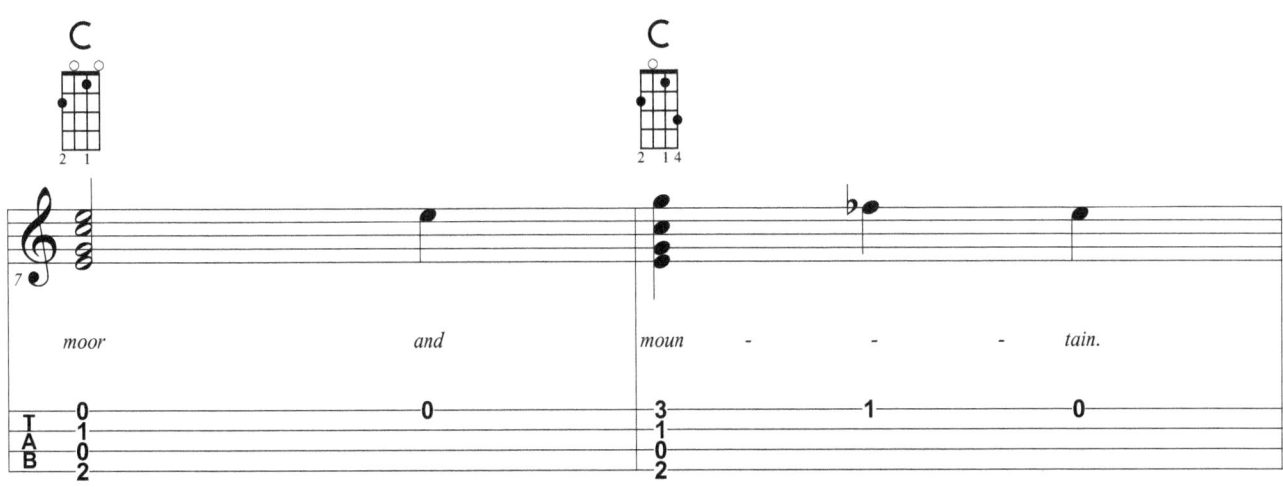
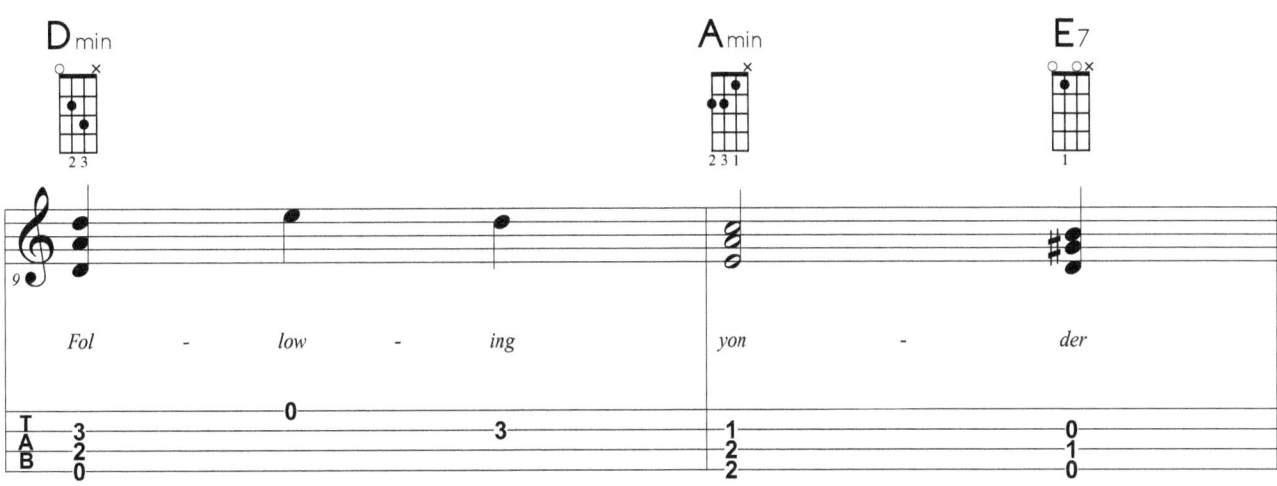
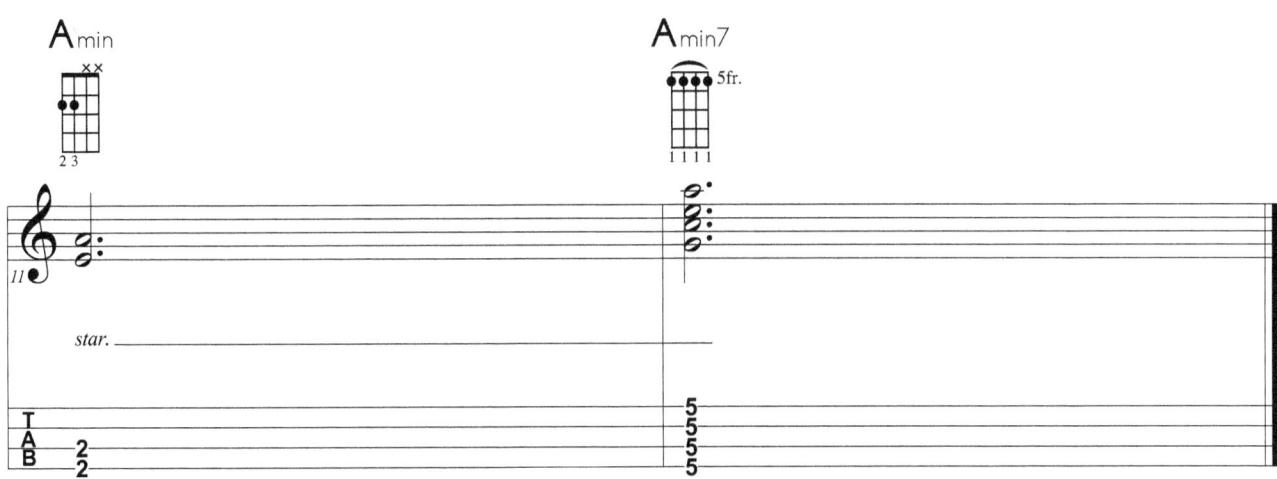

We Three Kings
Level 2
Page 1 of 2

In this version of the song, it is still in the key of A Minor but there is a continuous 1/8th note fingerpicking going on throughout the entire song. The trick to this version is to highlight the melody notes while playing the continuous fingerpicking.

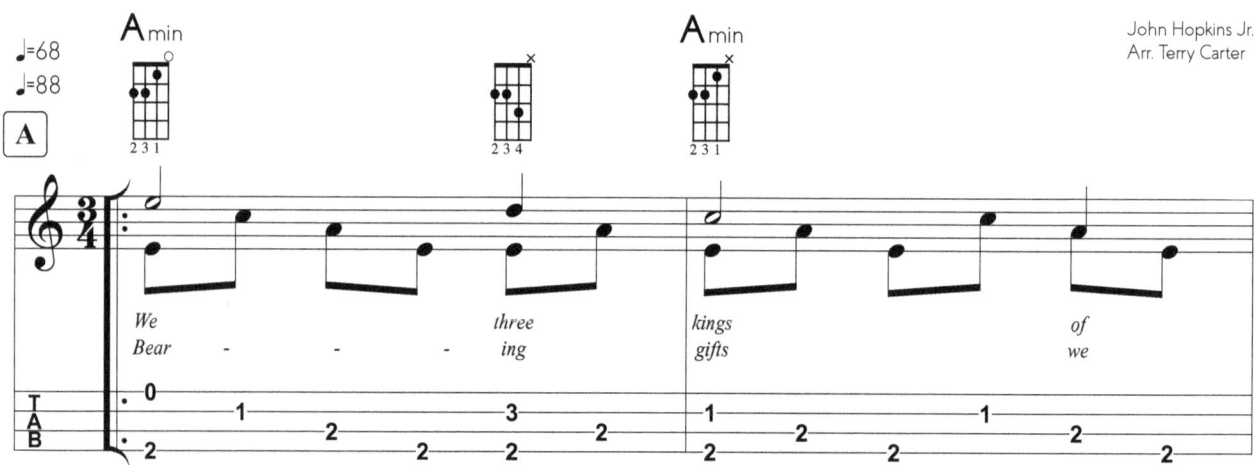

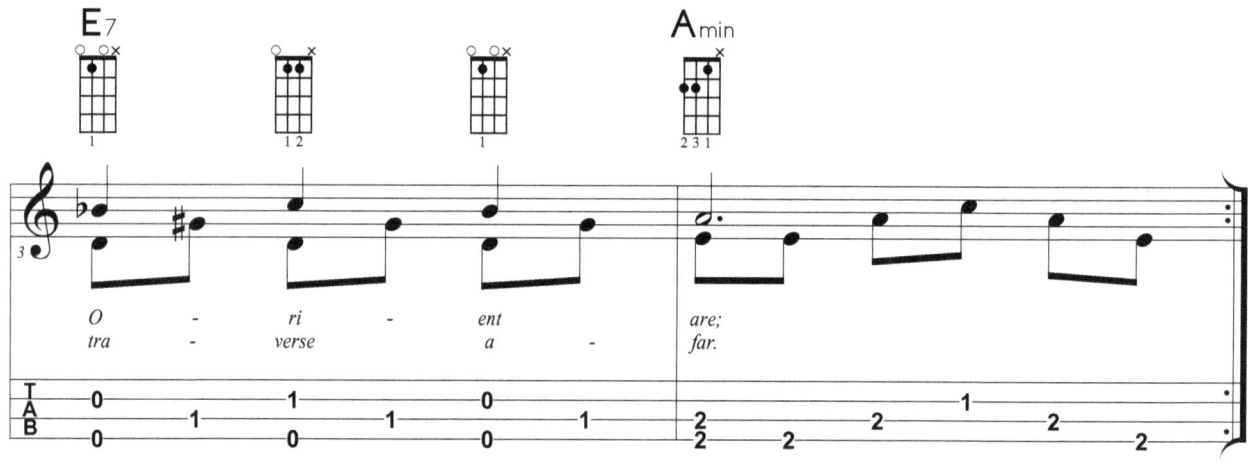

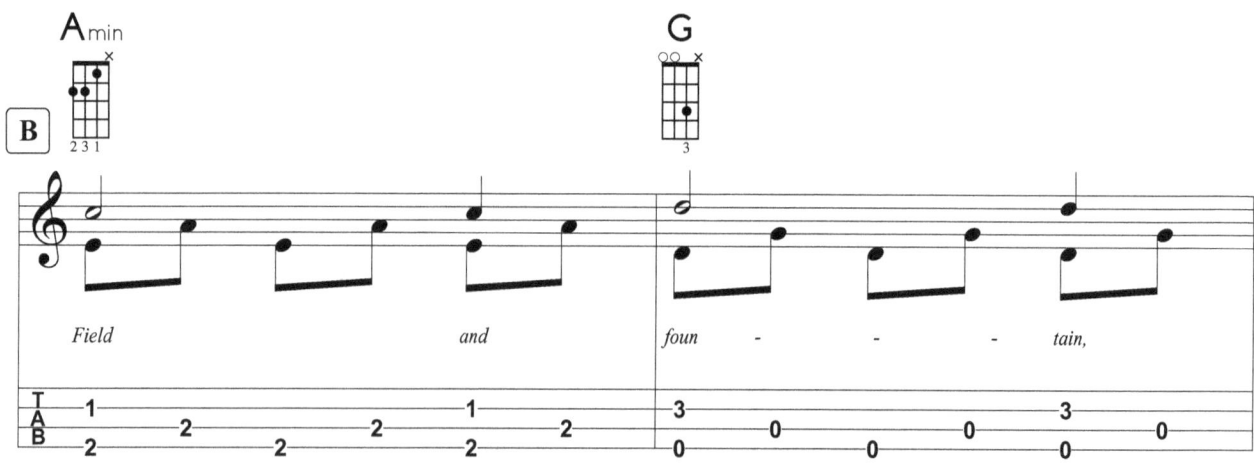

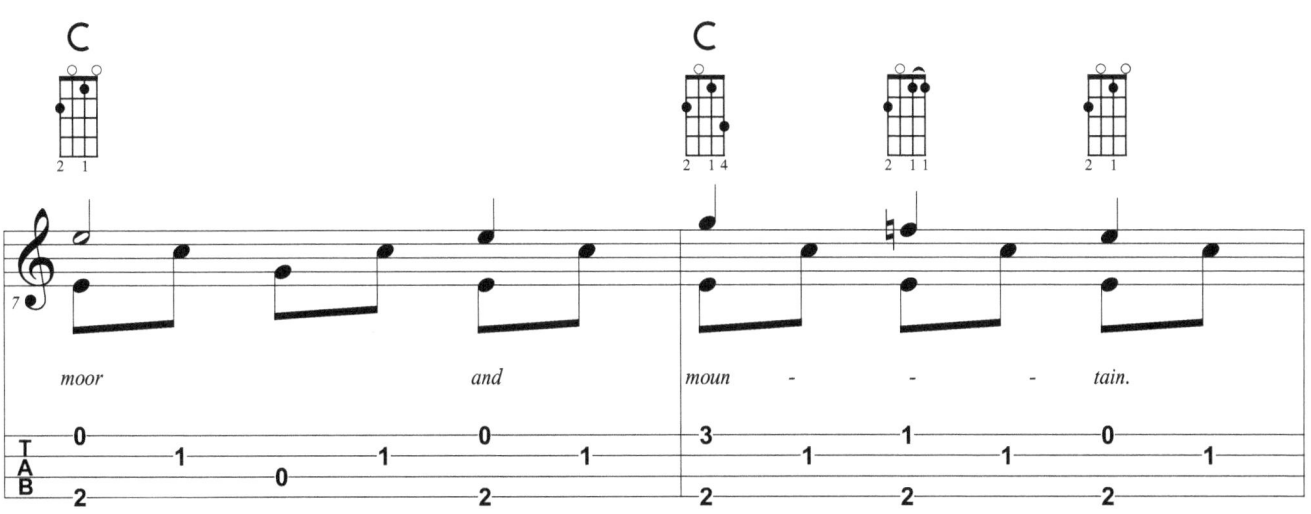
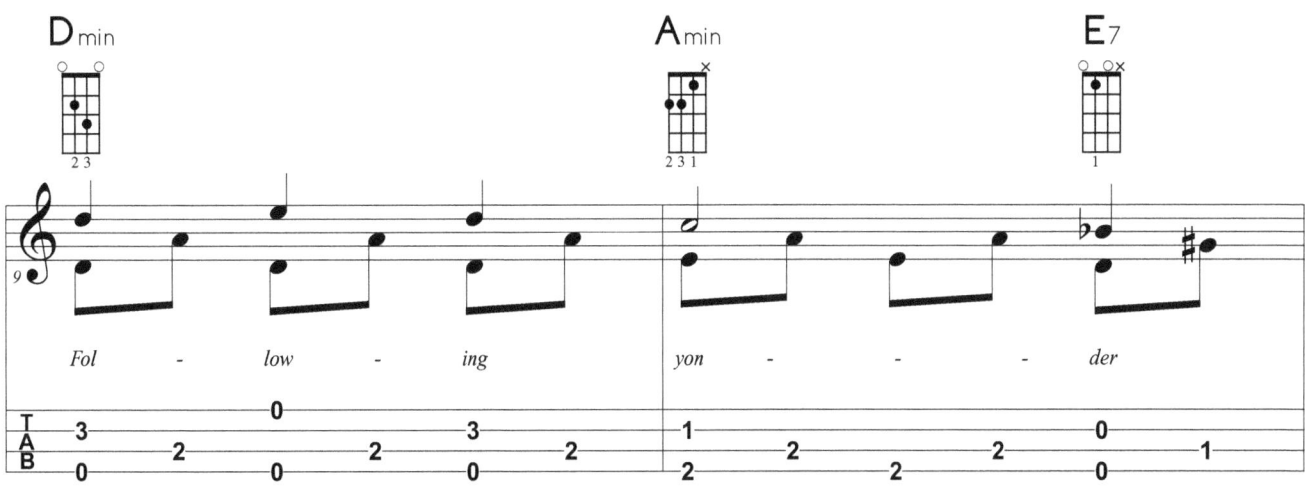
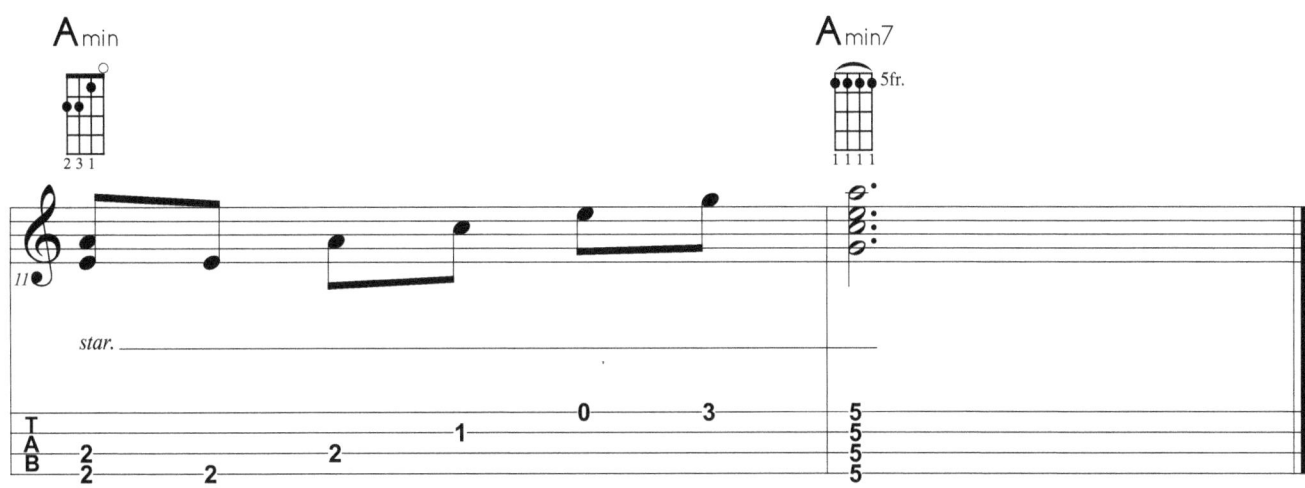

Silent Night

Page 1 of 2

This song is in 3/4 time and in the key of G Major. This arrangement creates some tension and release by the chord shapes used such as the 1st G chord, the G/#, and the different inversions of the D7 chords. There are some nice double stops (2 notes) in measure 18.

Joseph Mohr
Arr. Terry Carter

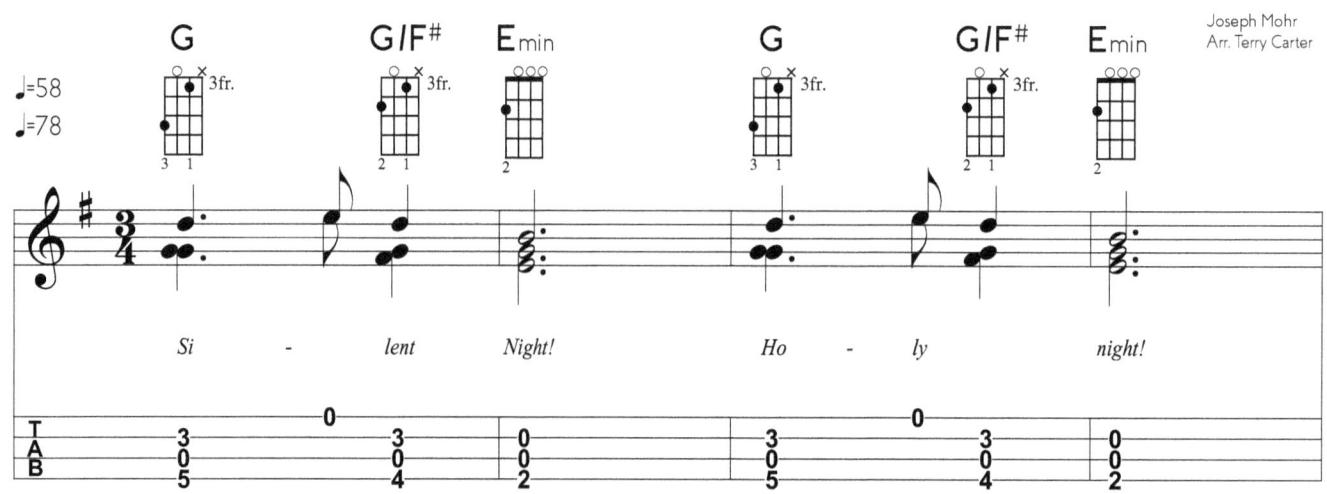

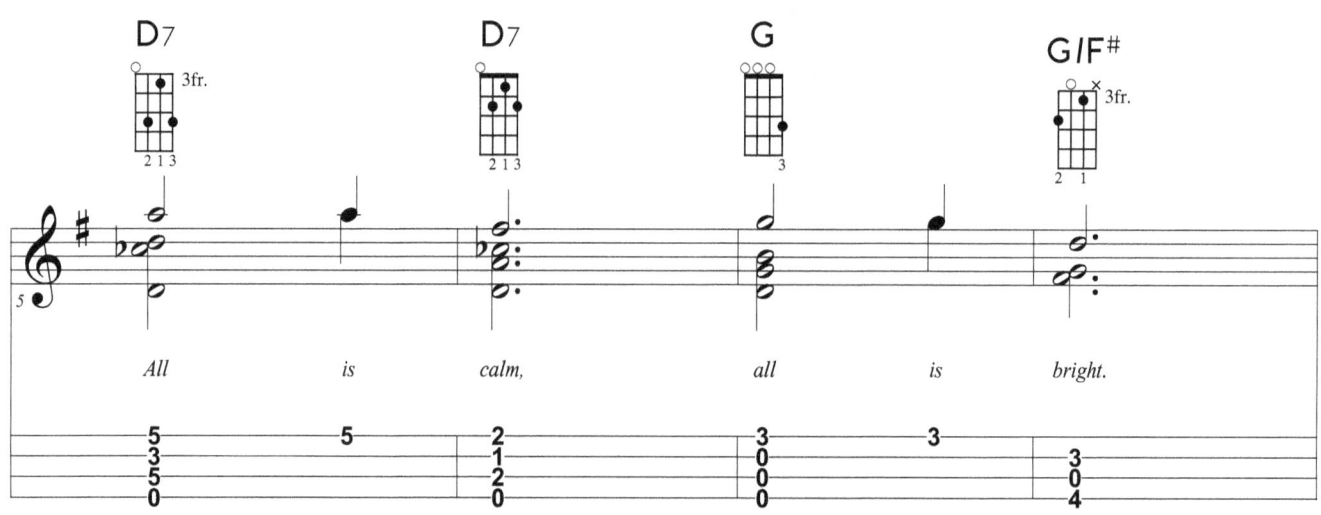

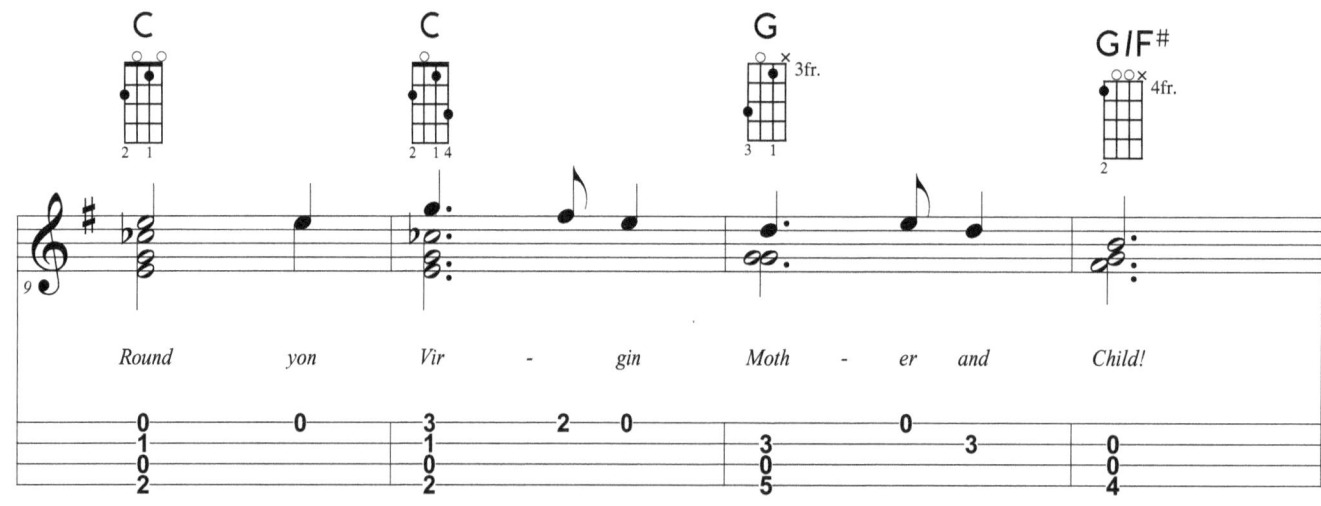

Silent Night

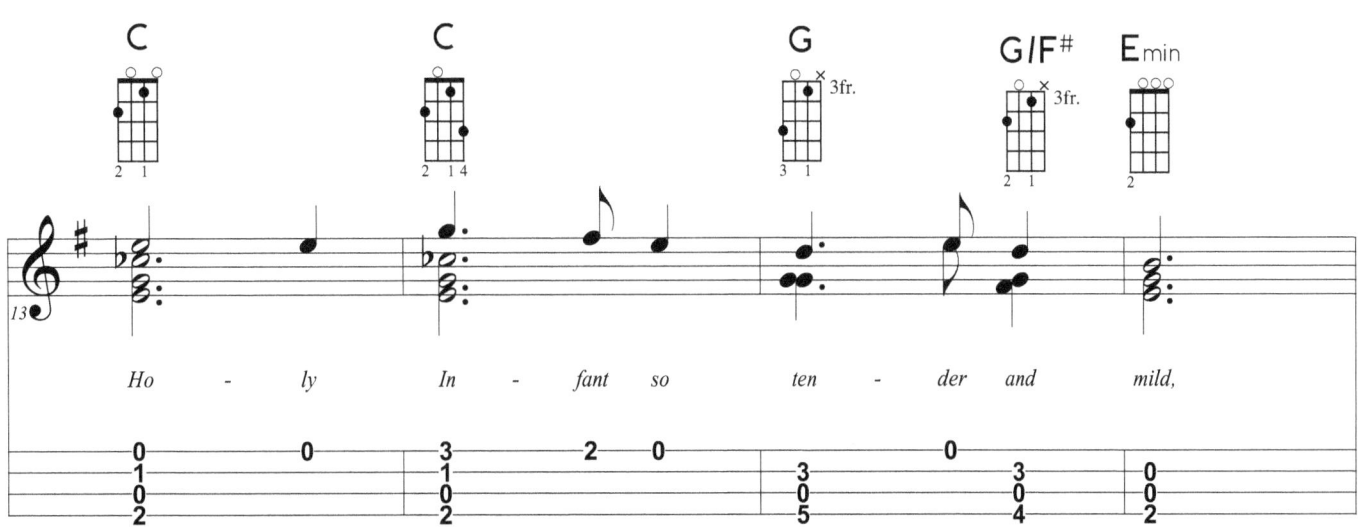
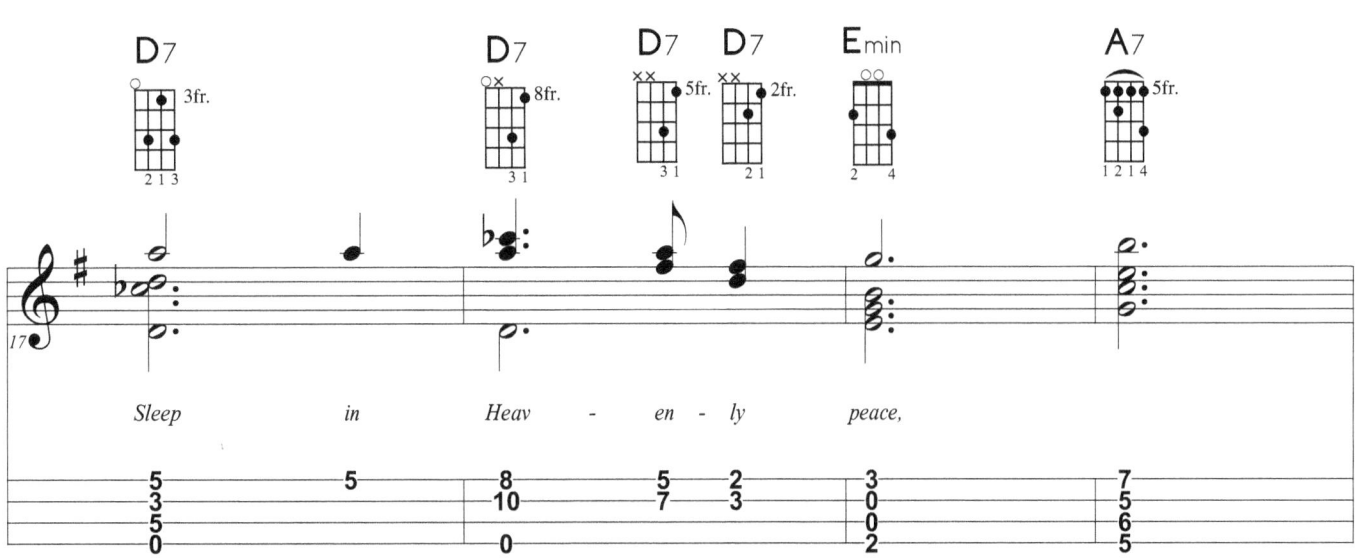
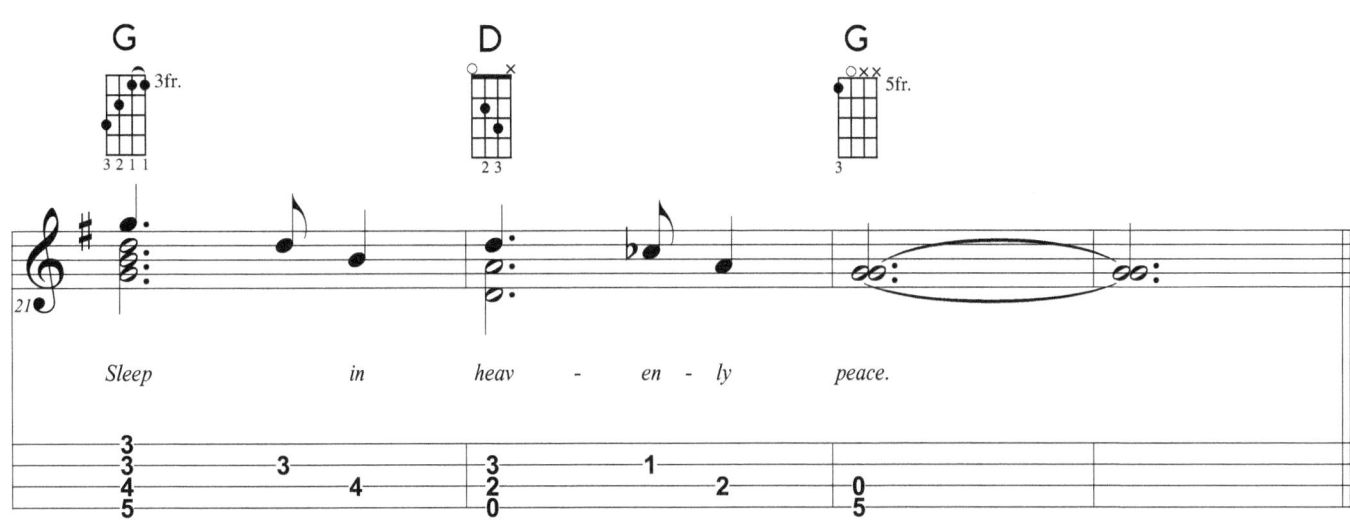

The Story Behind
SILENT NIGHT

"Silent Night" is one of the most famous and enduring Christmas carols, with a rich history that dates back to 1818. Written by Joseph Mohr, a young Austrian priest, the song's origins are both humble and heartfelt. The lyrics were penned as a poem by Mohr in 1816, and two years later, he approached his friend Franz Xaver Gruber, a local schoolteacher and organist, to compose a melody for the words. Together, they created the beautiful carol we know today, which was first performed on Christmas Eve at St. Nicholas Church in Oberndorf, Austria.

The story of the carol's creation is often described as a tale of necessity and inspiration. Legend has it that the church organ was broken, and Mohr wanted a simple song that could be accompanied by guitar for the Christmas Eve service. The resulting melody, combined with Mohr's gentle and hopeful lyrics, perfectly captured the spirit of the holiday—peace, love, and the birth of Jesus. "Silent Night" quickly spread throughout Austria and Germany, and eventually the world, becoming a beloved Christmas tradition.

The cultural significance of "Silent Night" cannot be overstated. The song has been translated into over 300 languages and is recognized by UNESCO as an intangible cultural heritage. During World War I, it famously played a role in the 1914 Christmas Truce, when soldiers on both sides of the Western Front laid down their arms, and the hauntingly beautiful melody of "Silent Night" echoed across the trenches, reminding everyone of their shared humanity even in the midst of conflict.

"Silent Night" has been recorded by countless artists, from classical choirs to popular singers like Bing Crosby, who recorded one of the best-selling versions of the carol. Its simple yet powerful message resonates with people of all ages and backgrounds, evoking a sense of peace and togetherness that transcends time and place. The gentle melody and poignant lyrics invite listeners to pause and reflect on the true meaning of Christmas—hope, love, and the promise of a better world.

One interesting fact about "Silent Night" is that it was declared a cultural treasure by UNESCO in 2011, recognizing its universal message of peace and its deep connection to the Christmas tradition. The carol's enduring popularity can be attributed to its simplicity and emotional depth, qualities that make it accessible and meaningful to people around the world. Whether sung in a grand cathedral, around a family Christmas tree, or even on a battlefield, "Silent Night" remains a powerful symbol of the holiday season, reminding us of the beauty of silence, reflection, and hope.

MASTER UKULELE
UKELIKETHEPROS.COM

O Come, O Come, Immanuel
Level 1
Page 1 of 3

This song is in 4/4 time, in the key of A Minor, and has a pickup note on beat 4. This is a great song for a chord melody arrangement because it's an active melody with lots of diatonic (moves by step) movement.

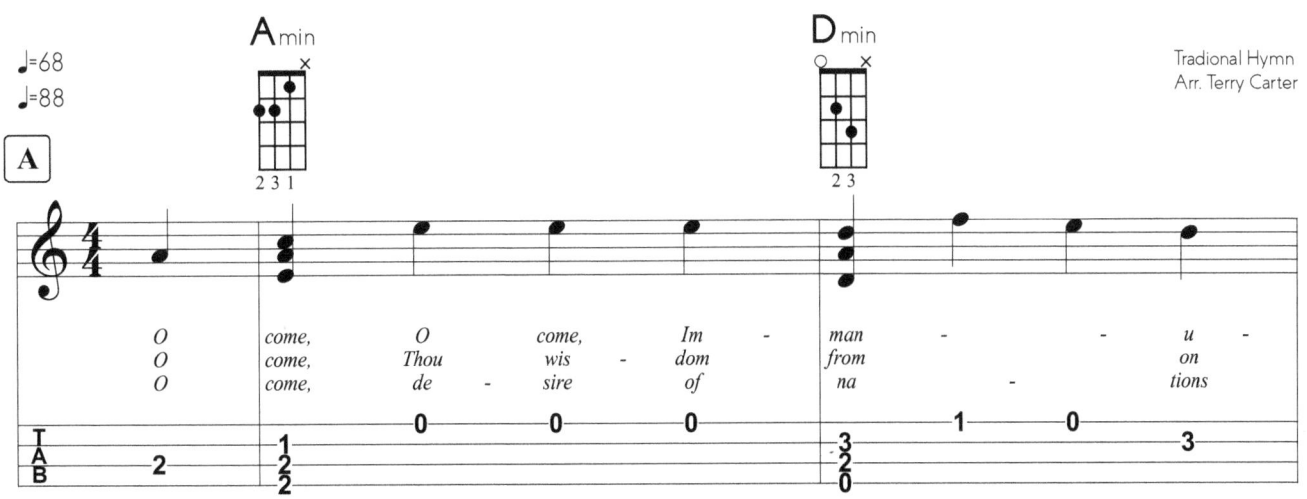

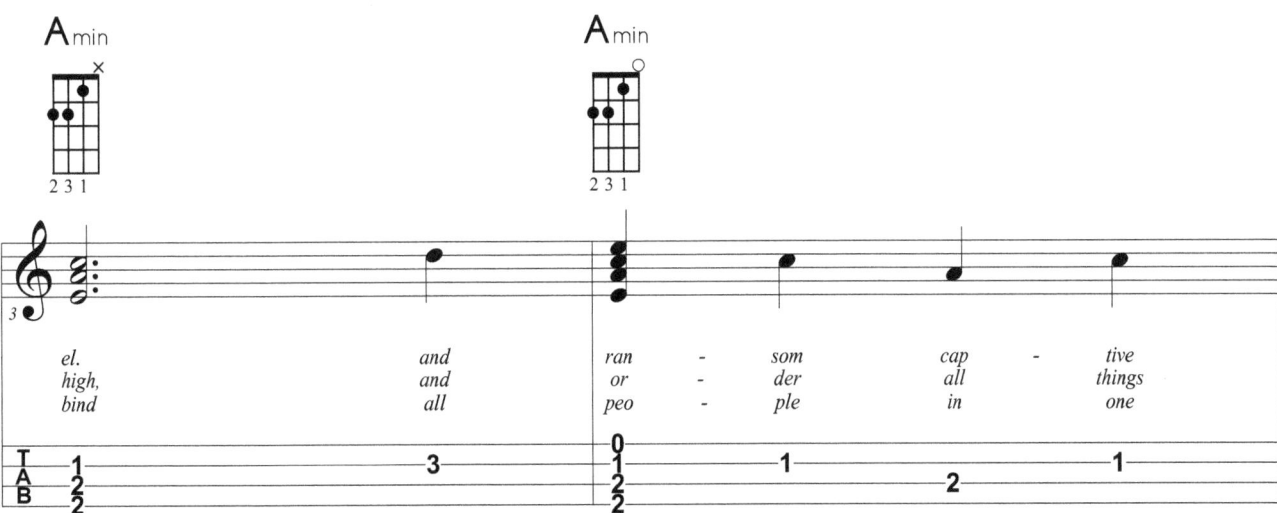

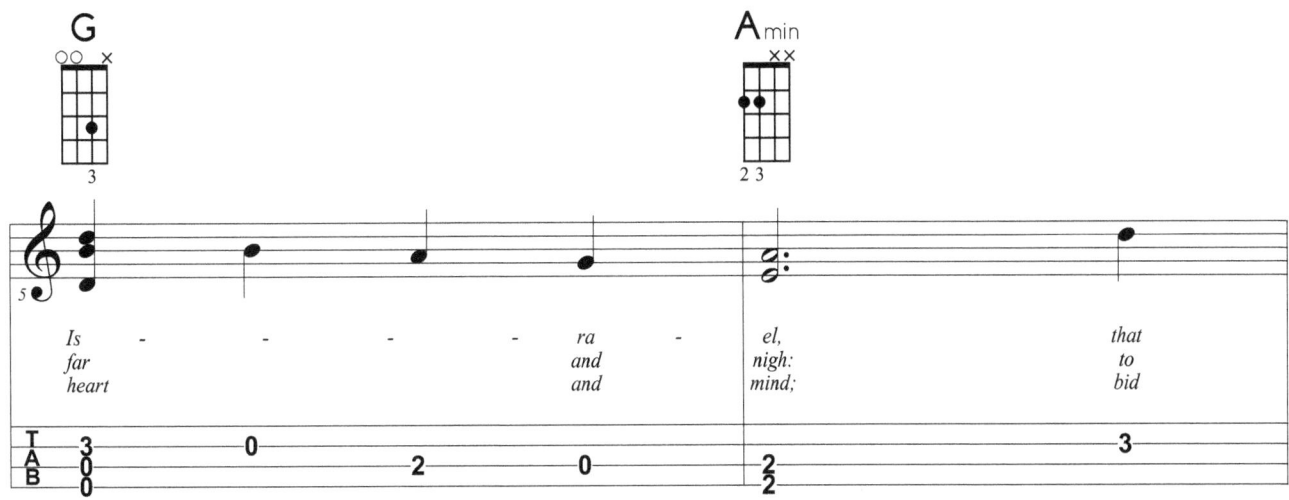

O Come, O Come, Immanuel Level 1

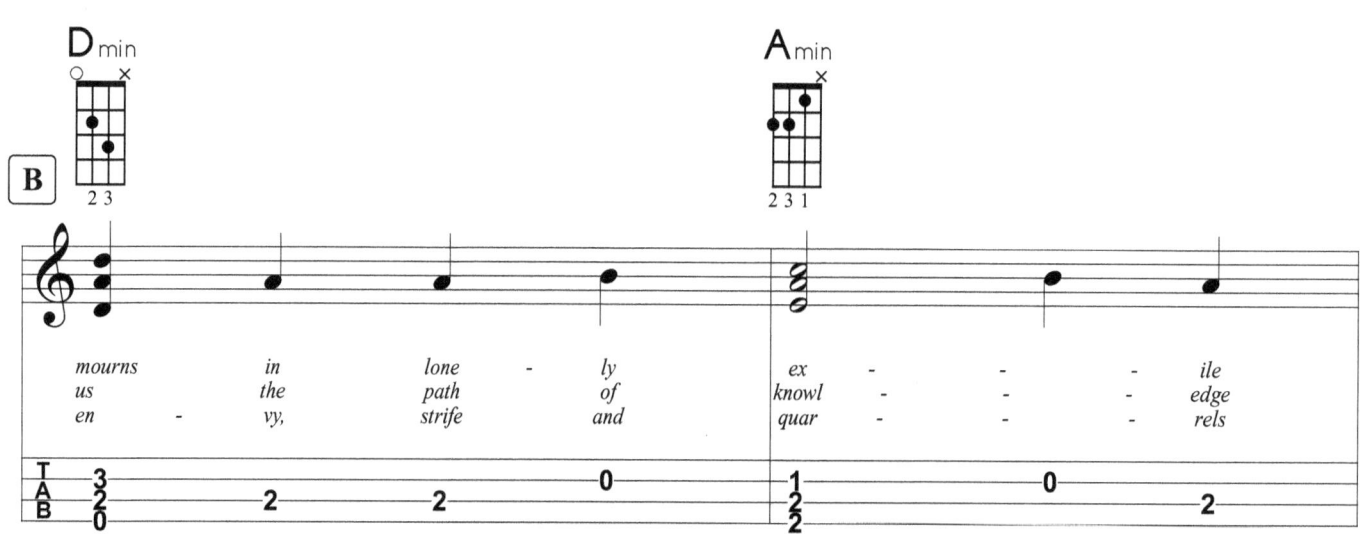
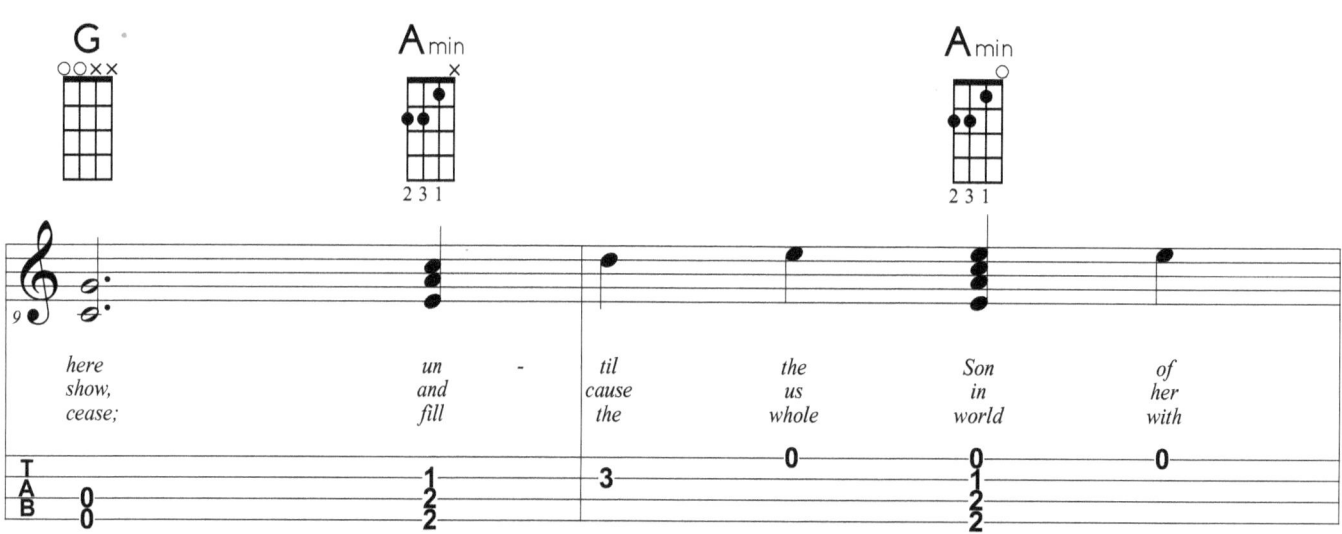
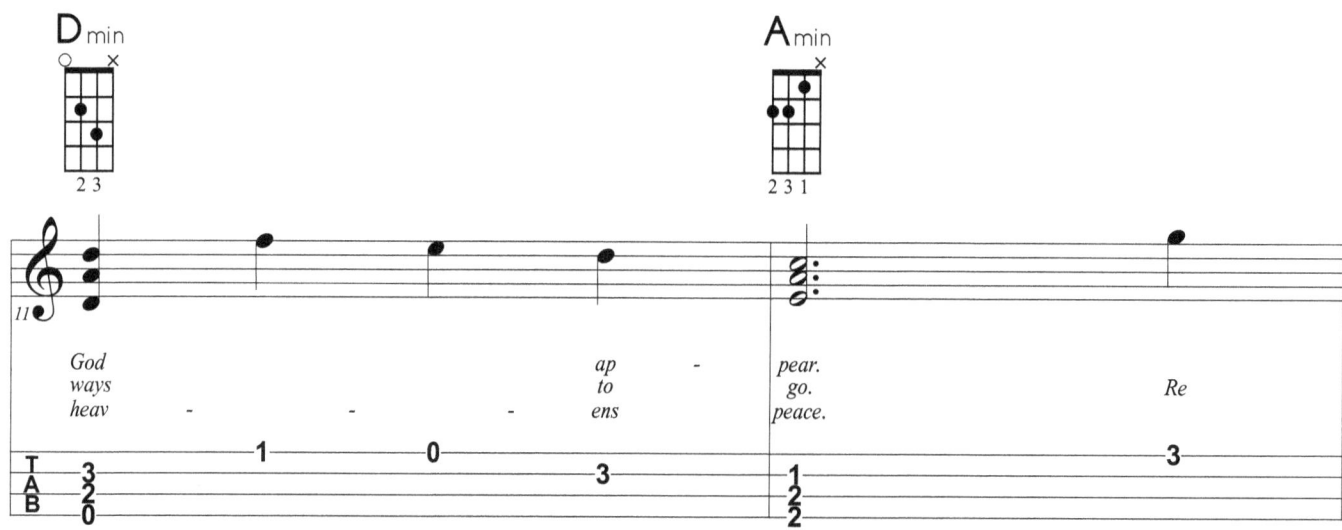

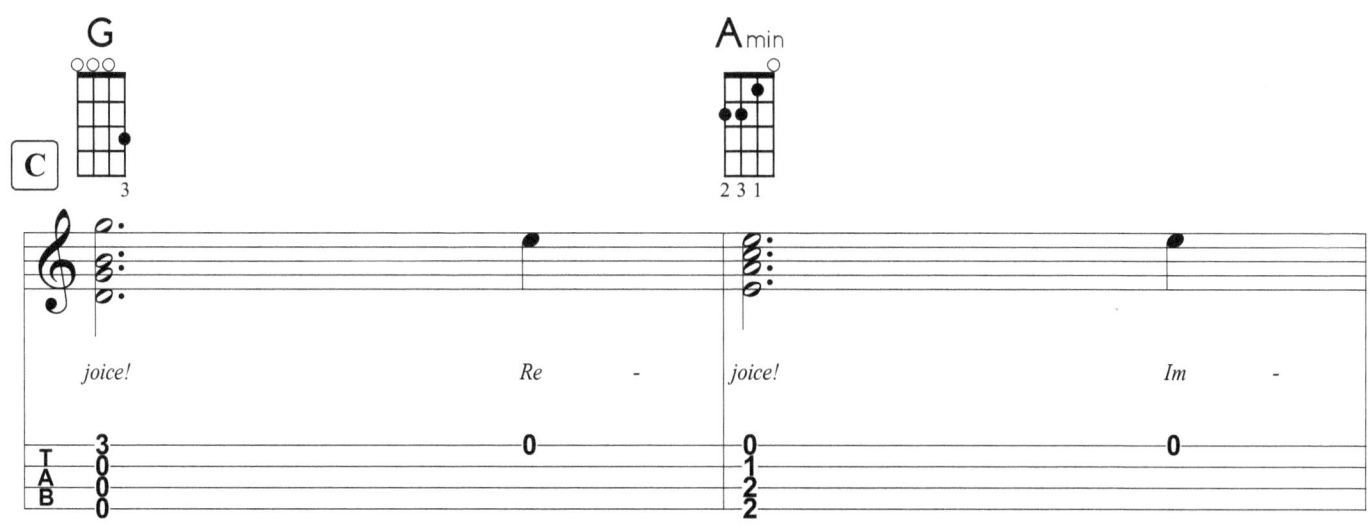
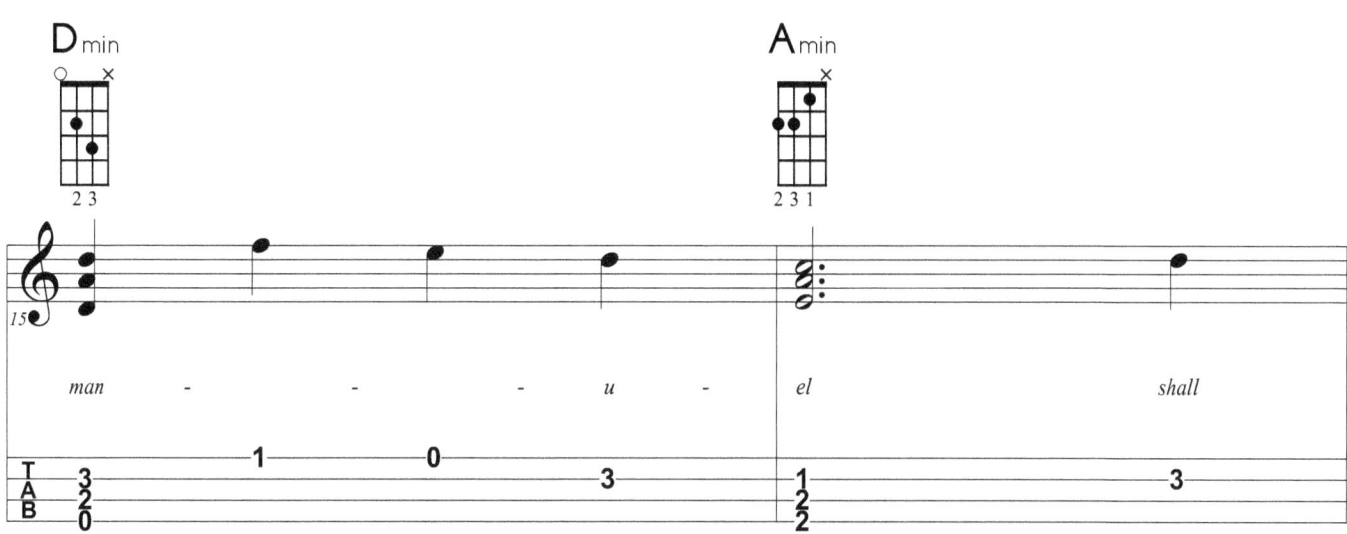
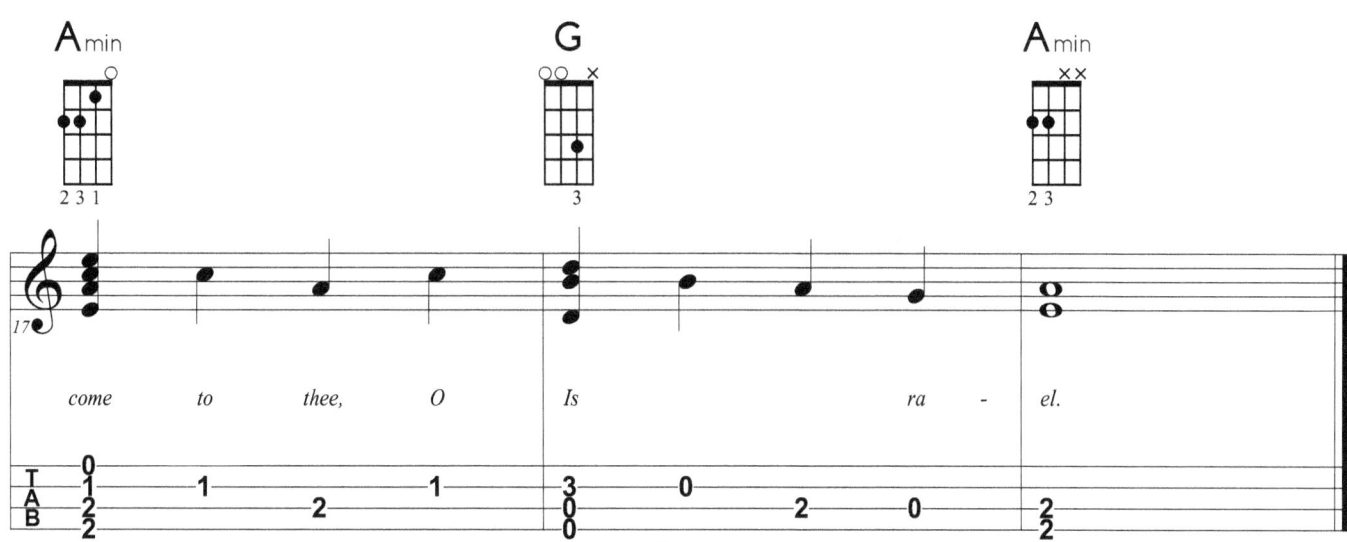

The Story Behind

O COME, O COME, IMMANUEL

"O Come, O Come, Immanuel" is one of the oldest and most cherished Advent hymns, with roots that trace back to the early medieval period. The lyrics are based on the "O Antiphons," a series of ancient Latin chants used in the liturgy of the Christian church during the week leading up to Christmas. These antiphons, which date back as far as the 8th or 9th century, each invoke a different title for the Messiah and express the longing of the people for a Savior. The hymn as we know it today was translated into English by John Mason Neale in the mid-19th century, bringing its rich and evocative imagery to a broader audience.

The haunting melody of "O Come, O Come, Immanuel" is believed to be of French origin and dates to the 15th century, though its exact origins are not entirely clear. The minor key of the melody gives the hymn a reflective, almost mournful quality, which contrasts beautifully with the hopeful anticipation expressed in the lyrics. The song captures the essence of Advent—a season of waiting, longing, and hope for the arrival of Christ. The repeated refrain, "Rejoice! Rejoice! Immanuel shall come to thee, O Israel," serves as a powerful reminder of the joy that awaits.

The cultural and spiritual significance of "O Come, O Come, Immanuel" lies in its expression of the human yearning for redemption and the fulfillment of God's promise. It embodies the deep desire for deliverance and peace, a theme that resonates beyond the context of Advent and speaks to the universal human condition. The hymn's connection to the "O Antiphons" links it directly to centuries of Christian tradition, giving it a sense of historical depth that few other carols possess.

"O Come, O Come, Immanuel" has been recorded by numerous artists, ranging from classical choirs to contemporary musicians. Its enduring appeal lies in its ability to evoke a sense of both solemnity and hope, making it a favorite during the Advent season. Artists such as Enya, Pentatonix, and Andrea Bocelli have offered their own interpretations, each highlighting the timeless and evocative quality of the hymn.

One interesting aspect of "O Come, O Come, Immanuel" is its dual nature—the juxtaposition of the somber verses with the hopeful, triumphant refrain. This reflects the dual nature of Advent itself: a time of both reflection and joyful anticipation. The hymn's powerful imagery, rooted in biblical prophecy, and its haunting melody have made it a beloved part of Christmas celebrations worldwide. It continues to invite listeners to reflect on the deeper meaning of the season, reminding us of the promise of salvation and the light that follows even the darkest of times.

ALL YOUR MUSIC NEEDS
TERRYCARTERMUSICSTORE.COM

O Come, O Come, Immanuel
Level 2
Page 1 of 3

This version is still in 4/4 time and in the key of A Minor with a pickup on beat 4. The biggest difference is that almost every melody note has a different chord attached to it giving the arrangement a more complex and rich sound. And it's harder to play as well.

Tradional Hymn
Arr. Terry Carter

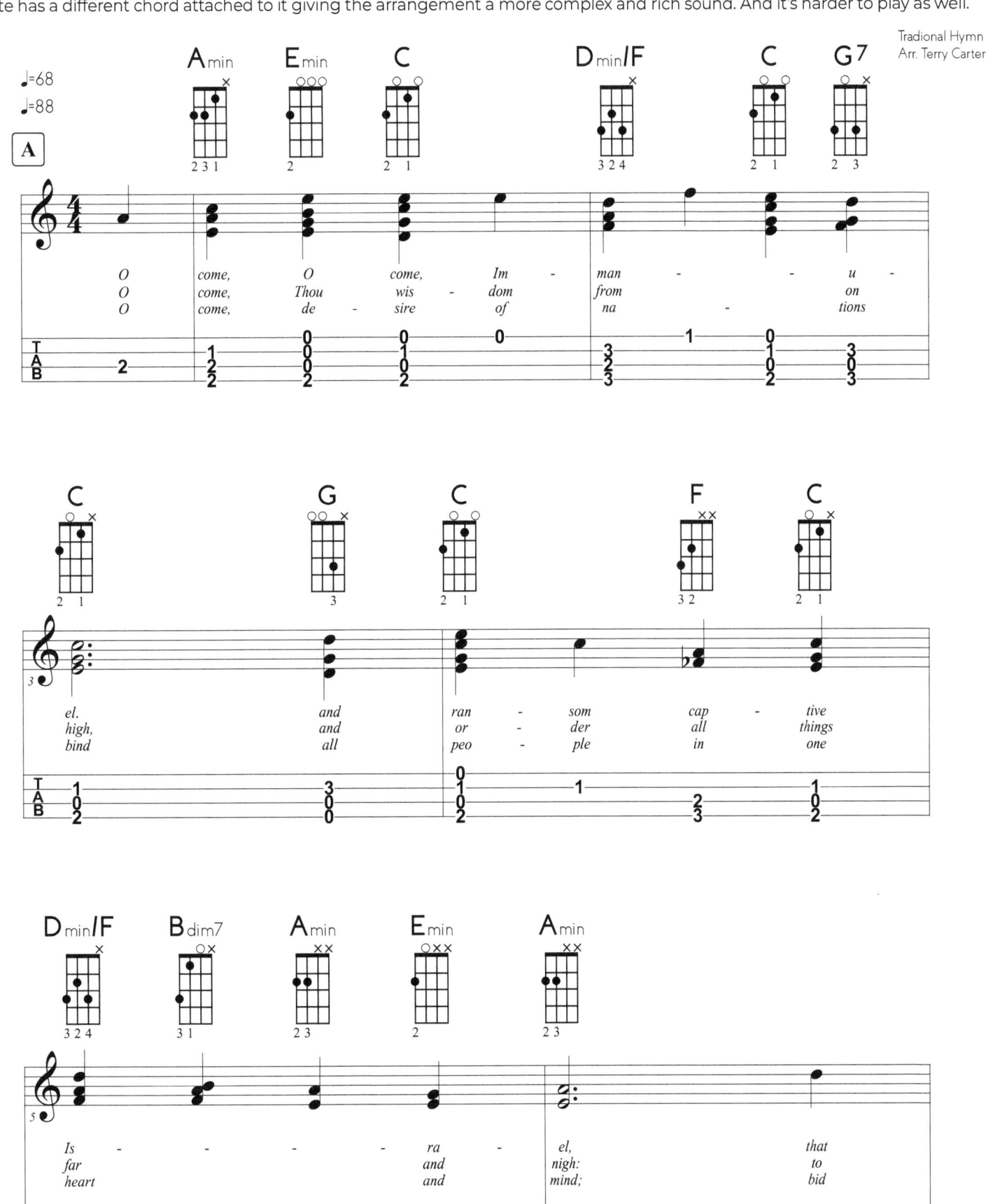

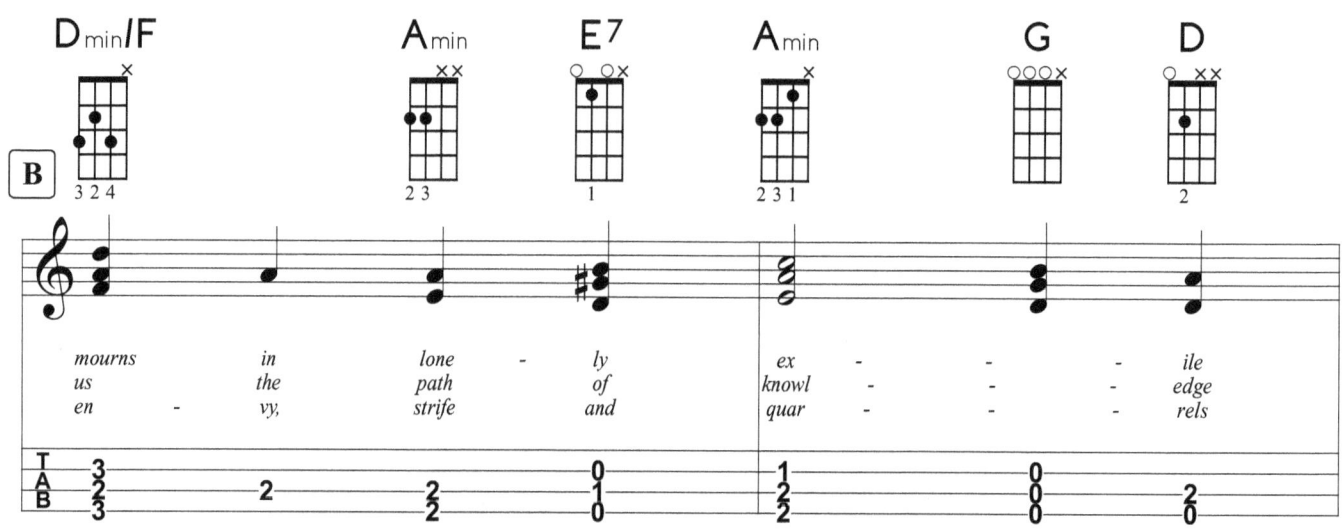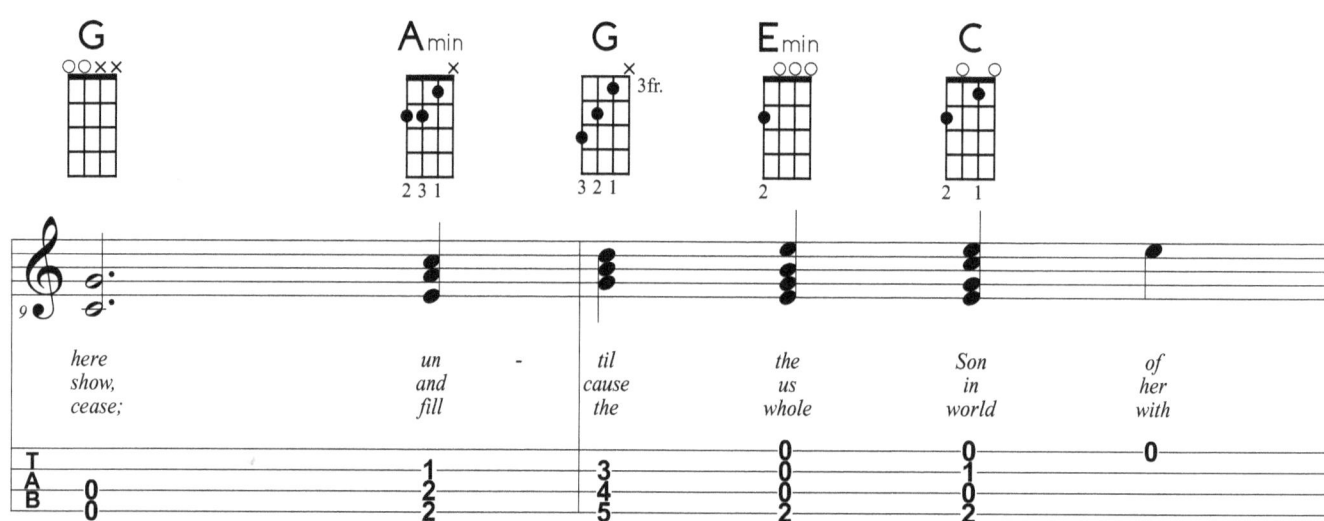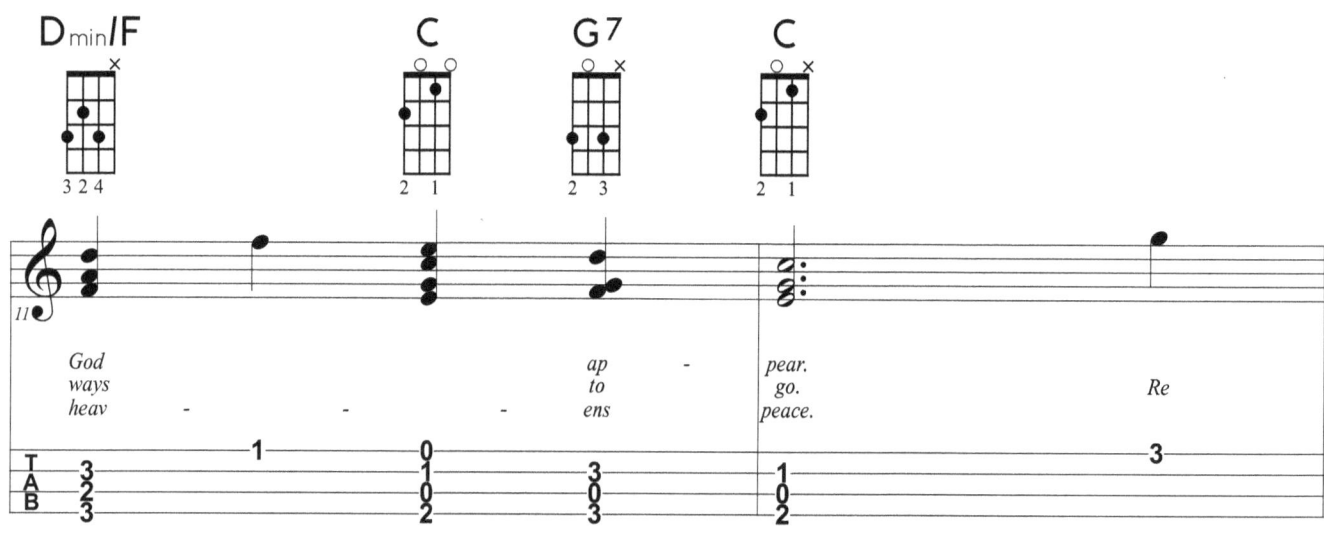

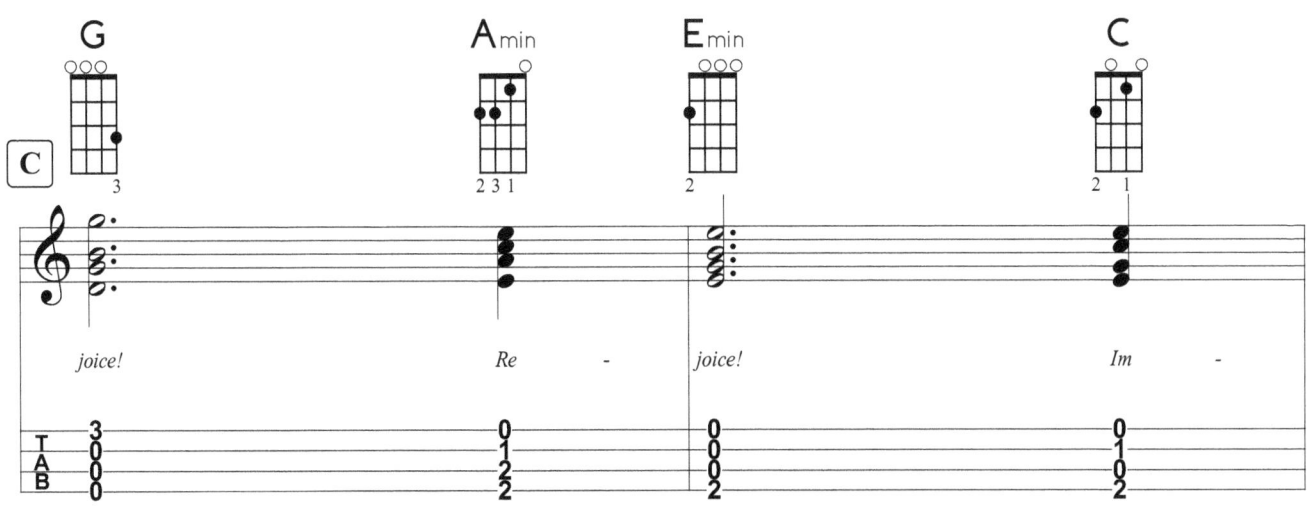
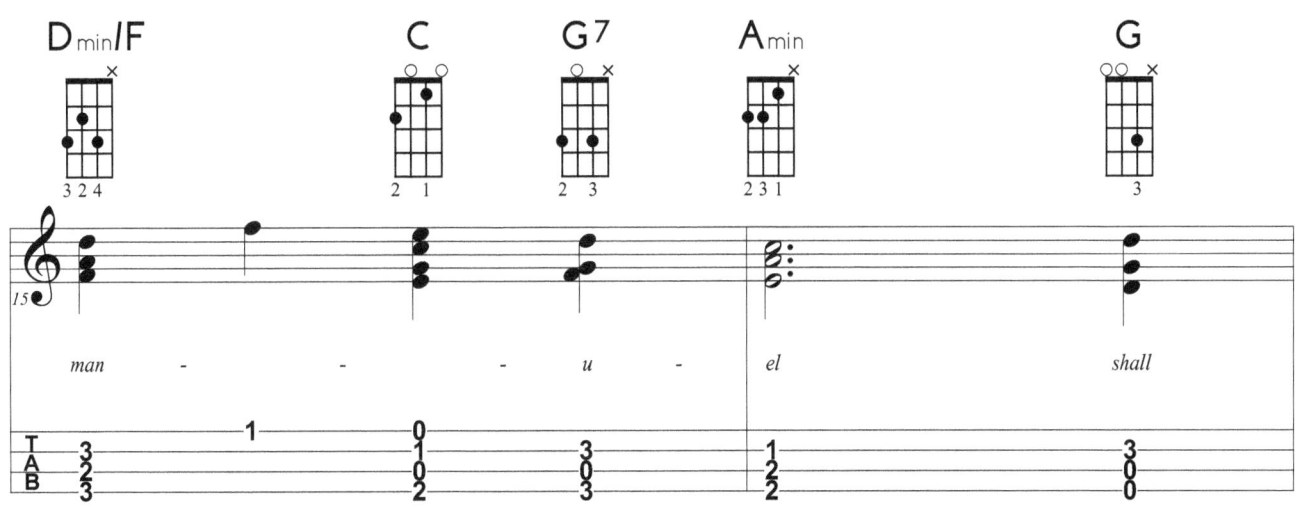
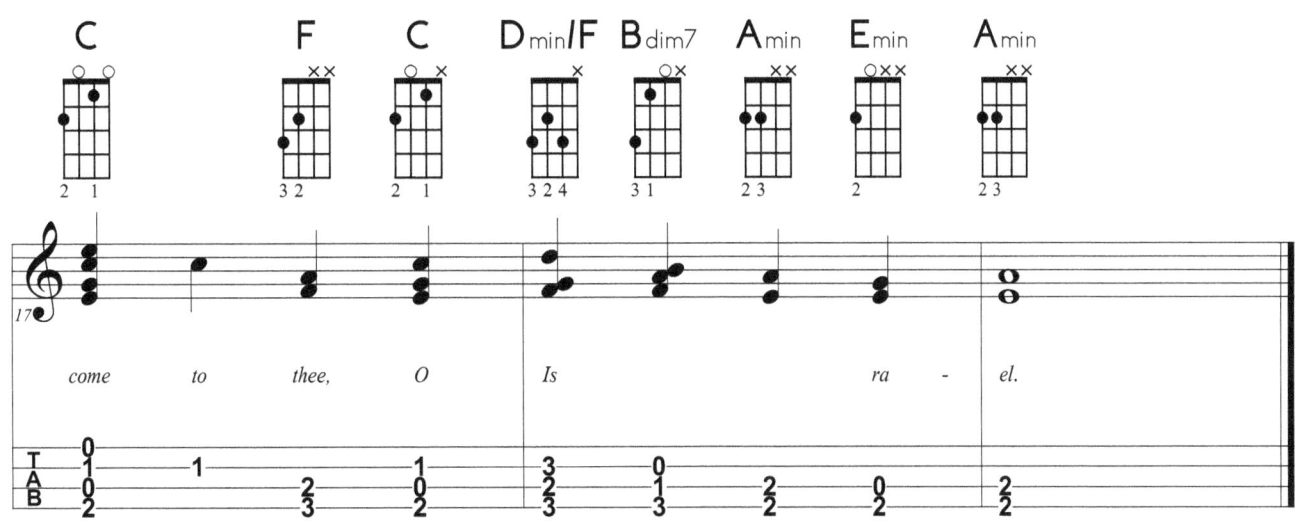

The First Noel
Page 1 of 2

This song is in 3/4 time, in the key of G Major, and starts with 1/8th note double stop pickup notes on beat 3. This piece uses beautifully voiced chords such as the Dadd4, D6, and Gadd9 chords. The arrangement ends in great sounding counterpoint (melody lines moving in opposite directions) in measures 21-22.

Tradional Hymn
Arr. Terry Carter

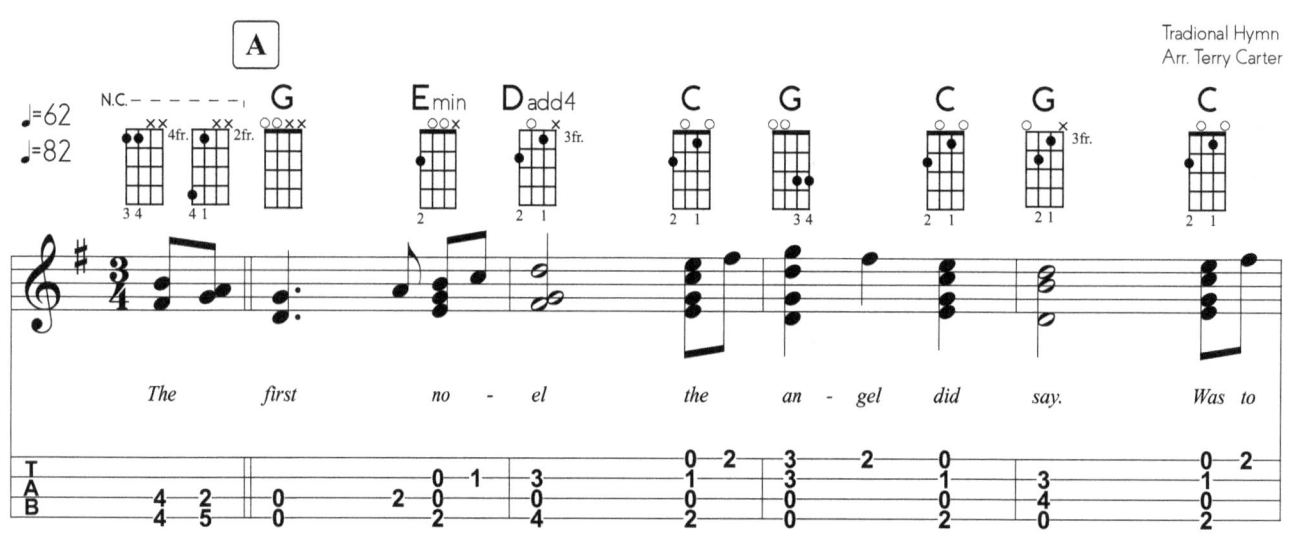
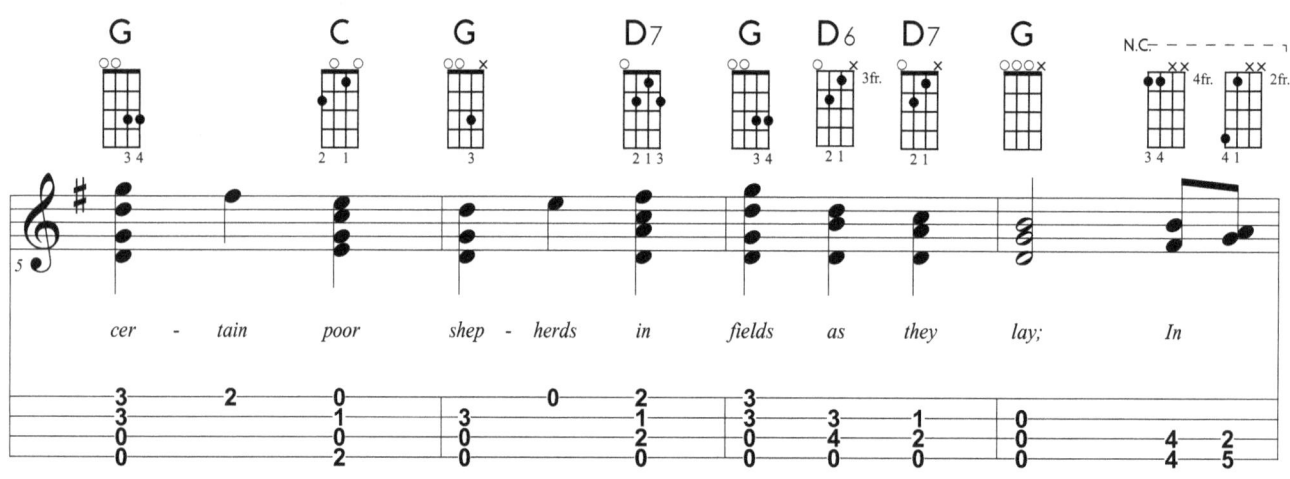
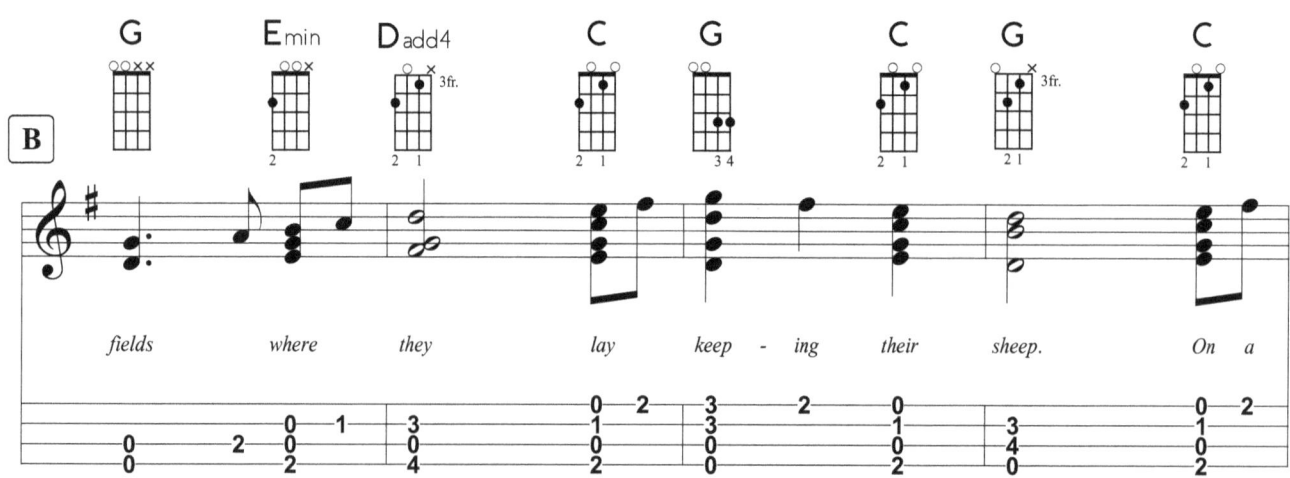

The First Noel

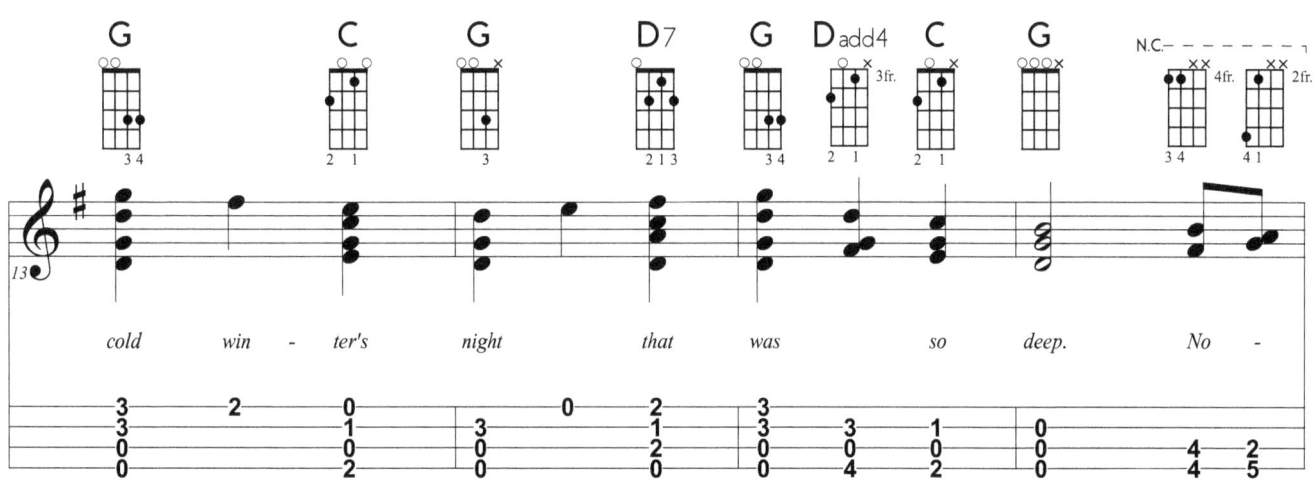
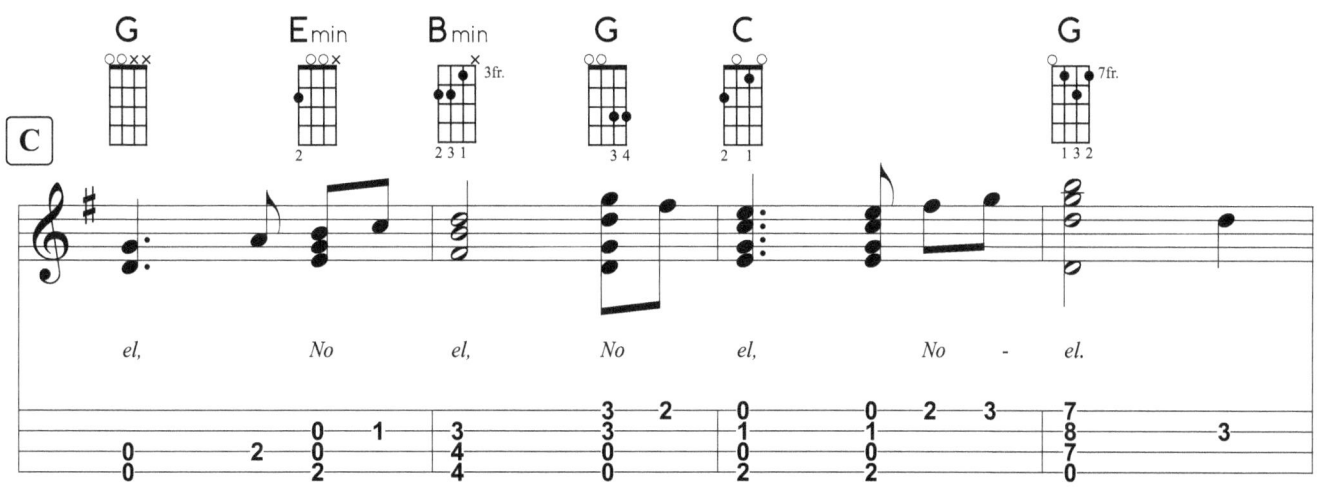
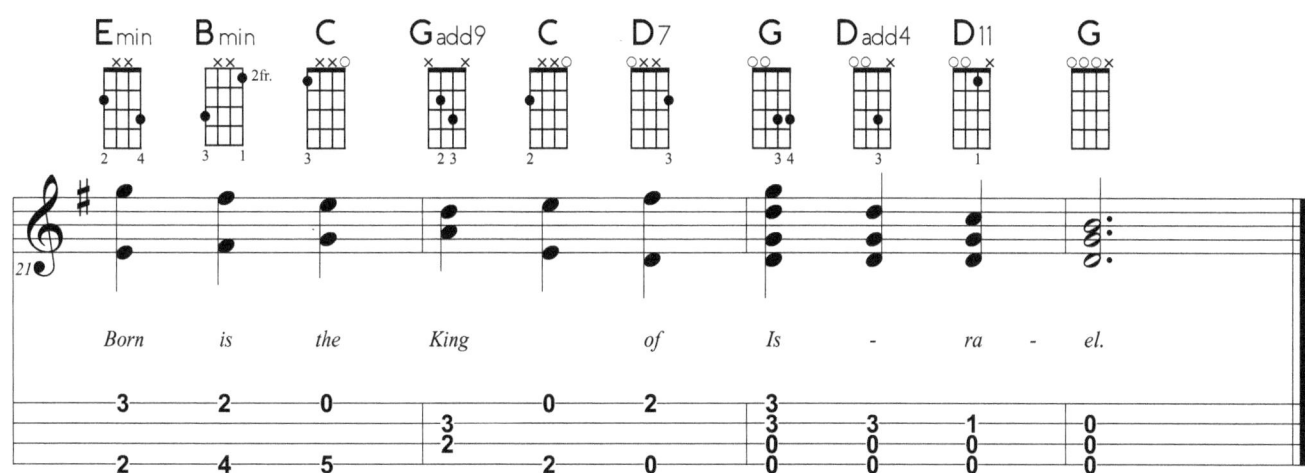

Deck The Halls
Page 1 of 2

This song is in 4/4 time and in the key of C Major. This arrangement uses a combination of double stop 3rds, bluesy 6ths, single notes, and some rich jazzy chords. This exact arrangement was used in Discount Tire commercials for several years.

Tradional
Arr. Terry Carter

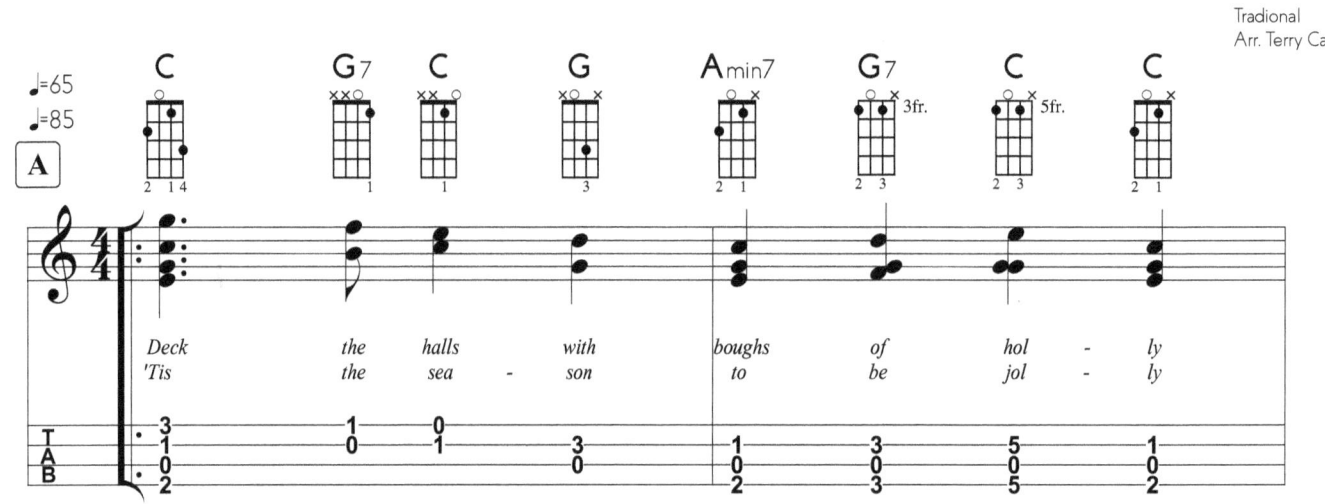

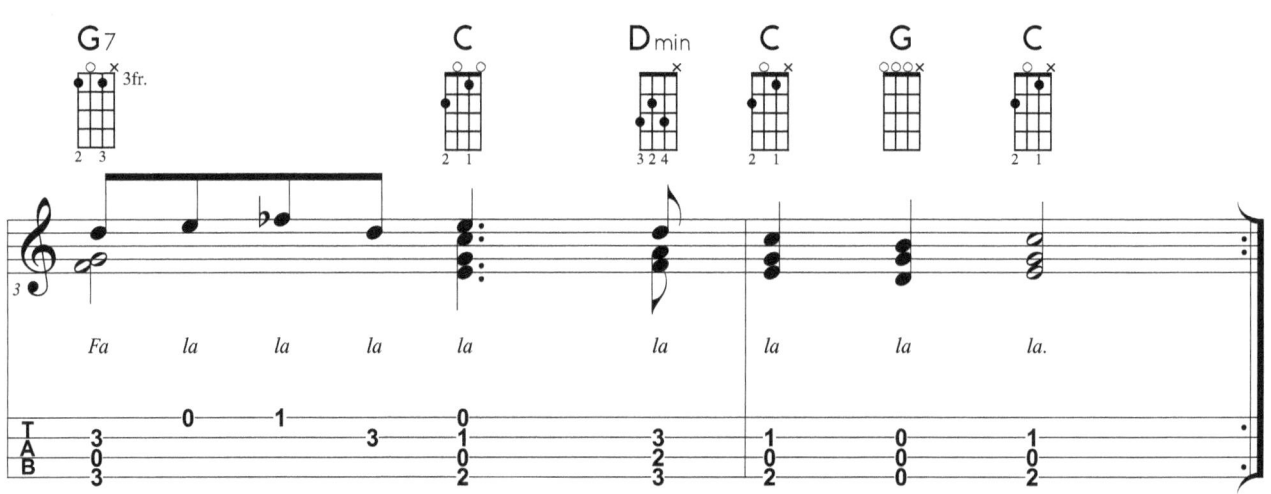

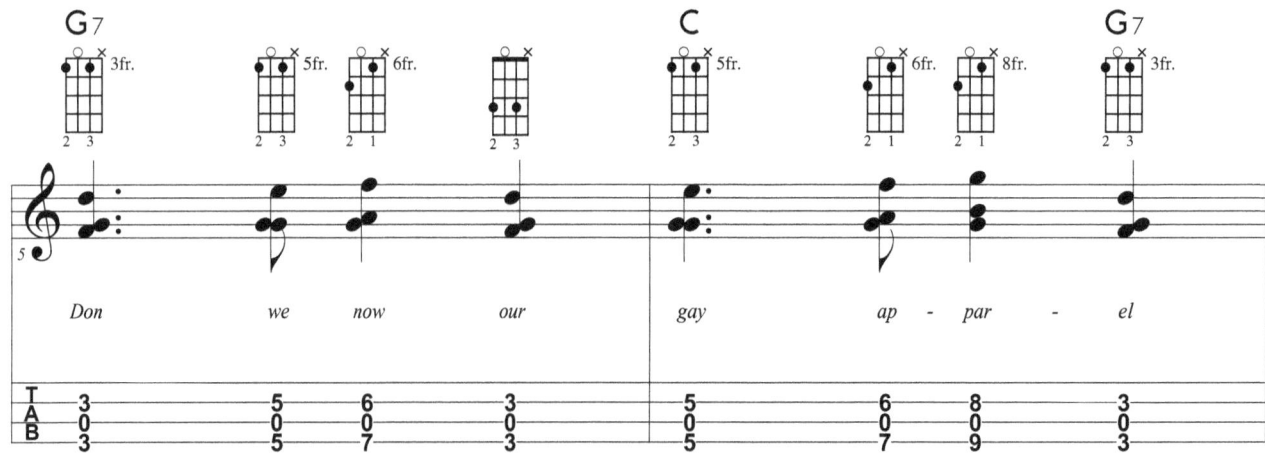

Deck The Halls

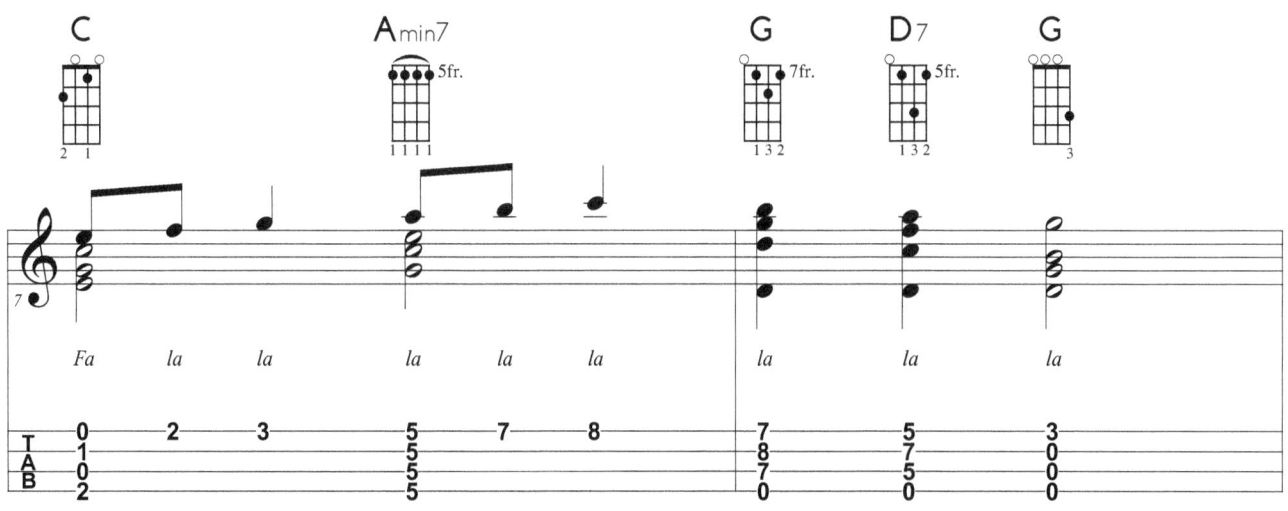
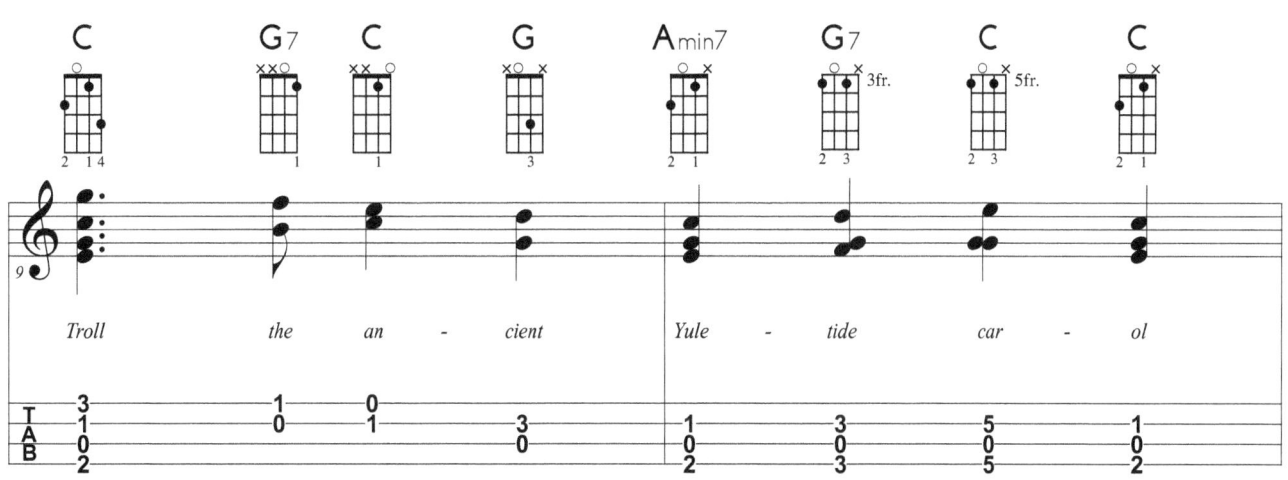
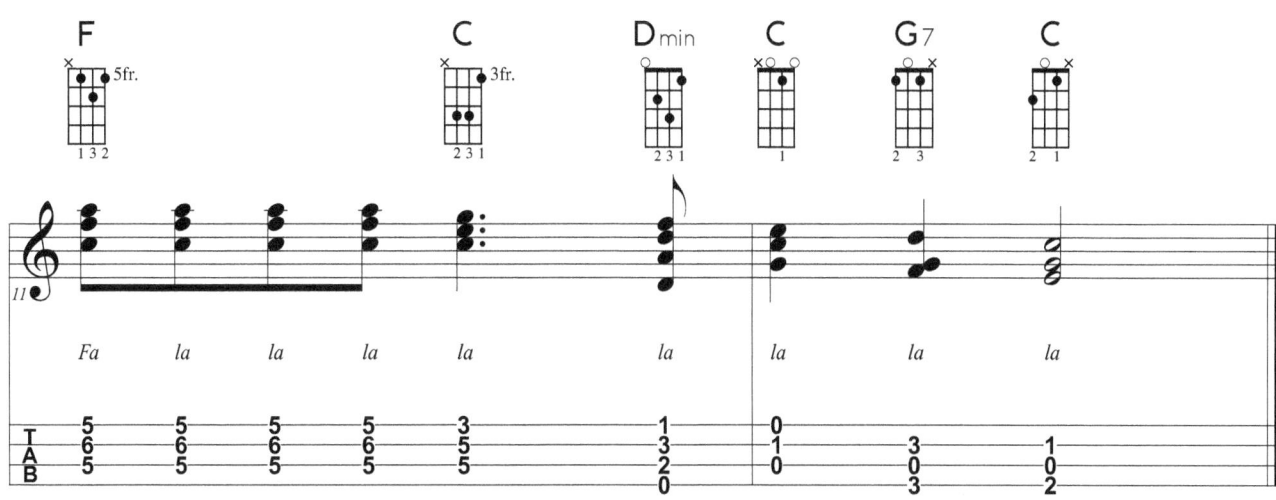

Jingle Bells

Page 1 of 2

This song is in 4/4 time and in the key of D Major. This arrangement is a sparse with not a lot of chords but uses single notes and double stops for the melody. There are some nice chord shapes including the E9, Dsus4, A9, and G5 chords.

James Pierpont
Arr. Terry Carter

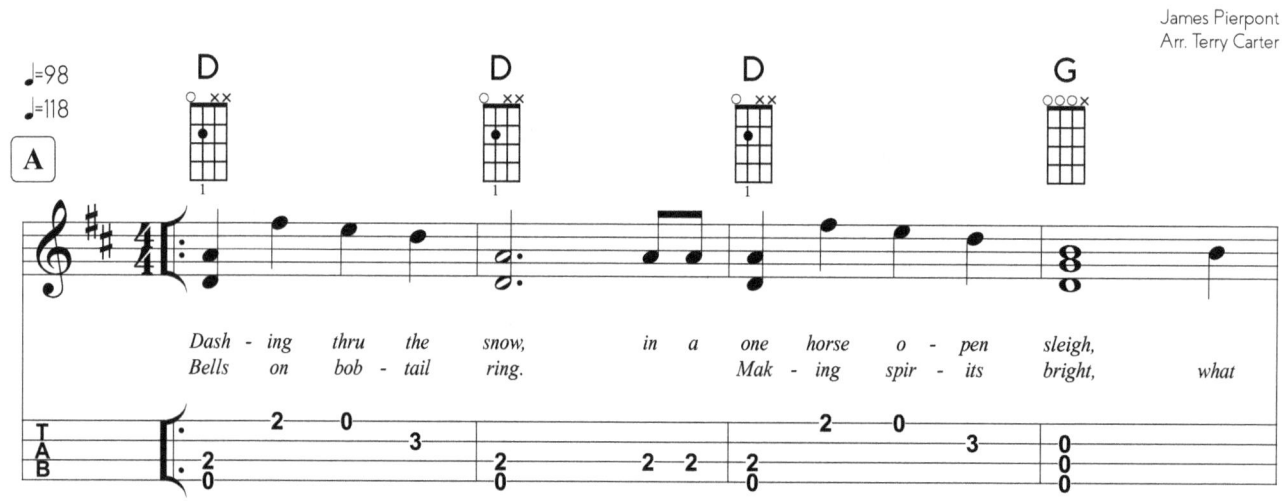

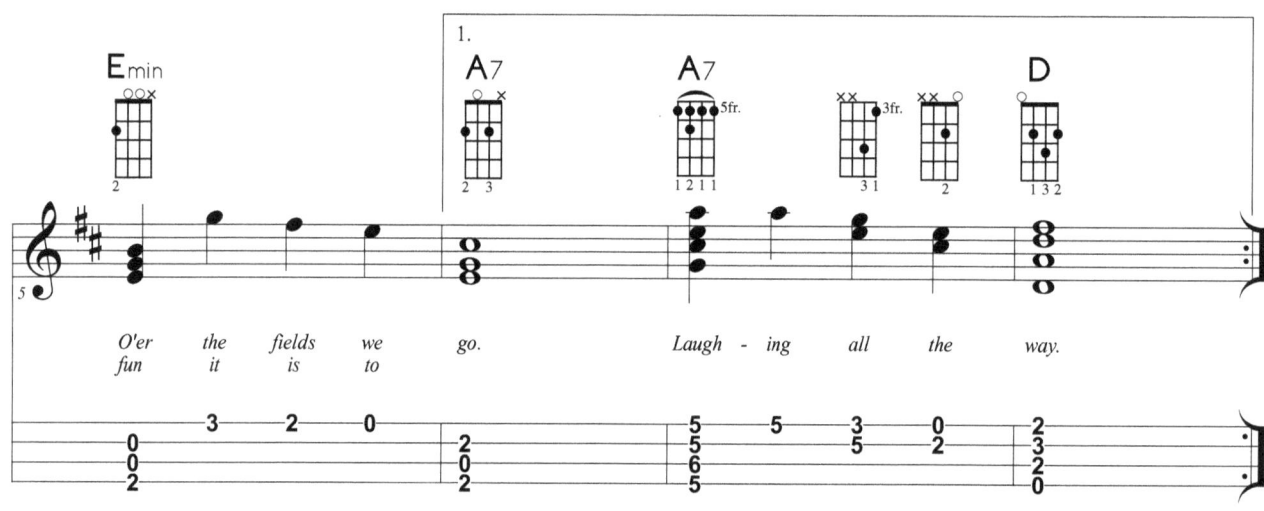

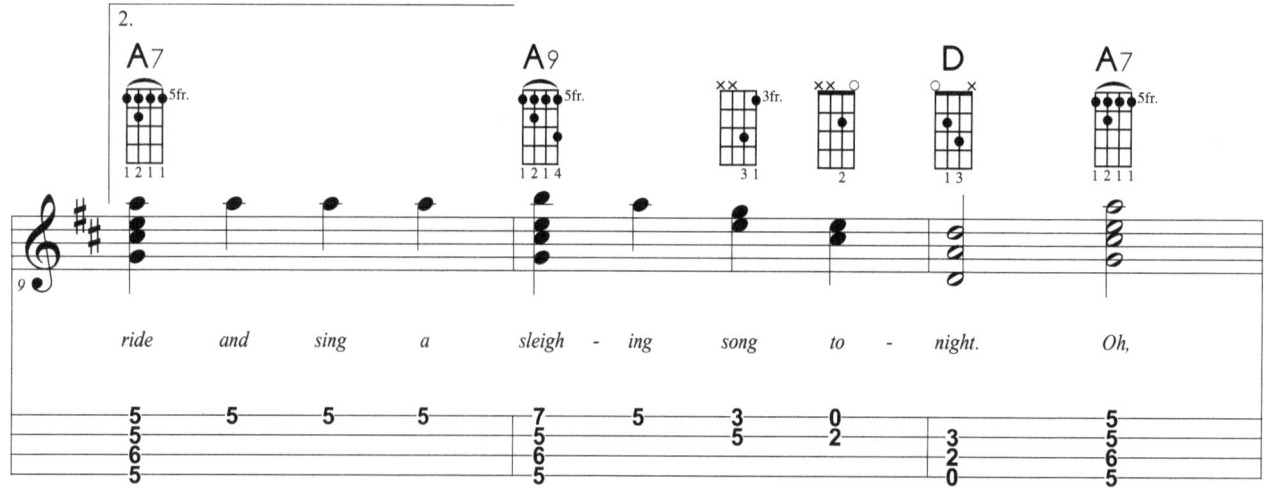

Jingle Bells

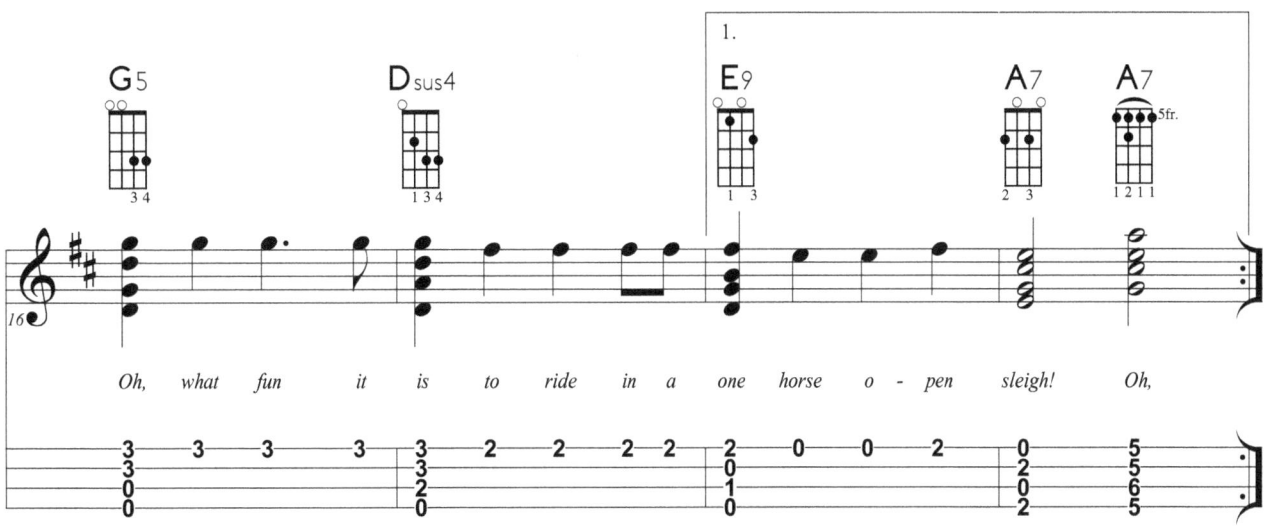
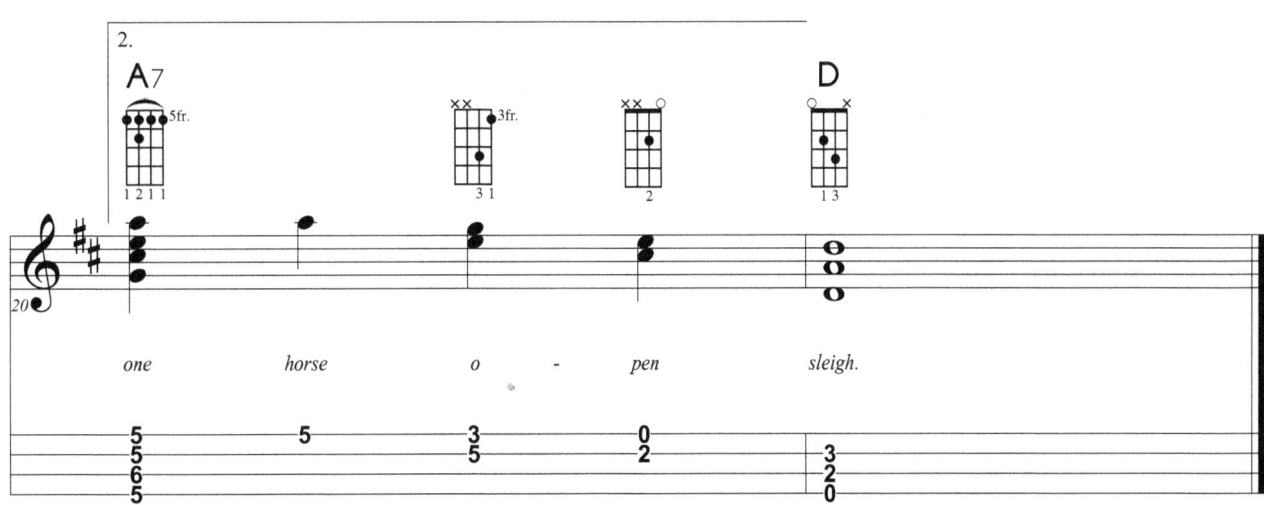

The Story Behind
JINGLE BELLS

"Jingle Bells" is one of the most well-known and beloved Christmas songs, originally composed by James Pierpont in 1857. Interestingly, the song was not initially intended to be a Christmas carol; it was written to celebrate the winter season and was originally titled "One Horse Open Sleigh." Pierpont, a songwriter and organist, composed the song while living in Savannah, Georgia, possibly inspired by the sleigh races that were popular in New England during the 19th century. The lively tune and catchy chorus quickly made it a favorite, and over time, it became associated with Christmas festivities.

The song's cheerful melody and lighthearted lyrics paint a picture of a joyful sleigh ride through the snow, evoking the fun and excitement of winter. The repeated refrain, "Jingle bells, jingle bells, jingle all the way," captures the carefree spirit of dashing through the snow and the laughter shared with friends. Its simple, memorable tune makes it easy to sing along to, which is part of the reason it has remained so popular for over a century. Today, it is almost impossible to imagine a Christmas season without hearing "Jingle Bells" played on the radio, in shopping malls, or at holiday gatherings.

One fascinating aspect of "Jingle Bells" is that it was the first song ever broadcast from space. In December 1965, astronauts Tom Stafford and Wally Schirra aboard NASA's Gemini 6 mission played the song using a harmonica and sleigh bells, which they had brought along as a light-hearted surprise. This playful moment brought a bit of holiday cheer to space exploration and further cemented the song's place in popular culture.

"Jingle Bells" has been recorded by countless artists across multiple genres, from classic renditions by Bing Crosby and Frank Sinatra to more modern interpretations by artists like Michael Bublé and Gwen Stefani. Its infectious rhythm and joyful lyrics make it a favorite for both children and adults, and it has been adapted into various languages and musical styles worldwide.

Despite its association with Christmas, the lyrics of "Jingle Bells" never actually mention the holiday itself. Instead, the song focuses on the simple pleasures of wintertime fun—riding in a sleigh, the crisp winter air, and the joy of being with friends. This universality is part of what has made "Jingle Bells" so enduring; it celebrates the joy of the season in a way that is inclusive and relatable to people everywhere, regardless of their specific holiday traditions.

"Jingle Bells" continues to be a beloved part of the holiday season, embodying the fun and festivity of winter. Its catchy melody and light-hearted lyrics invite everyone to join in the spirit of the season, reminding us all of the joy that can be found in simple pleasures, laughter, and shared experiences during this special time of year.

MASTER GUITAR
ROCKLIKETHEPROS.COM

SANTA CLAUS
is coming
TO TOWN

Scan this QR code to access a special video tutorial, backing track and exclusive printable for 'Santa Claus Is Coming To Town.' This private lesson is our gift to you, only for those who have this book. Get ready to play along and add even more Holiday cheer to your playing!

GREAT JOB!

Congratulations on completing the Uke Like The Pros Christmas Baritone Ukulele Fingerstyle Chord Melody book by Terry Carter! You've shown dedication to improving your skills and deepening your musical understanding. Through this journey, you've gained a stronger grasp of Christmas music, fingerstyle techniques, and chord melodies on the baritone ukulele.

You're now a more confident player with better timing, feel, technique, and expression. To continue your growth, consider taking the next step by becoming a Platinum Member at **ukelikethepros.com/platinum**. As a Platinum Member, you'll have access to over 40 courses, workshops, challenges, exclusive giveaways, and live practice sessions with the supportive ULTP community.

Give yourself the gift of ongoing improvement—become a Platinum Member today!

The Essentials

It is important to learn and memorize these terms and symbols because they not only apply to ukulele but to all music.

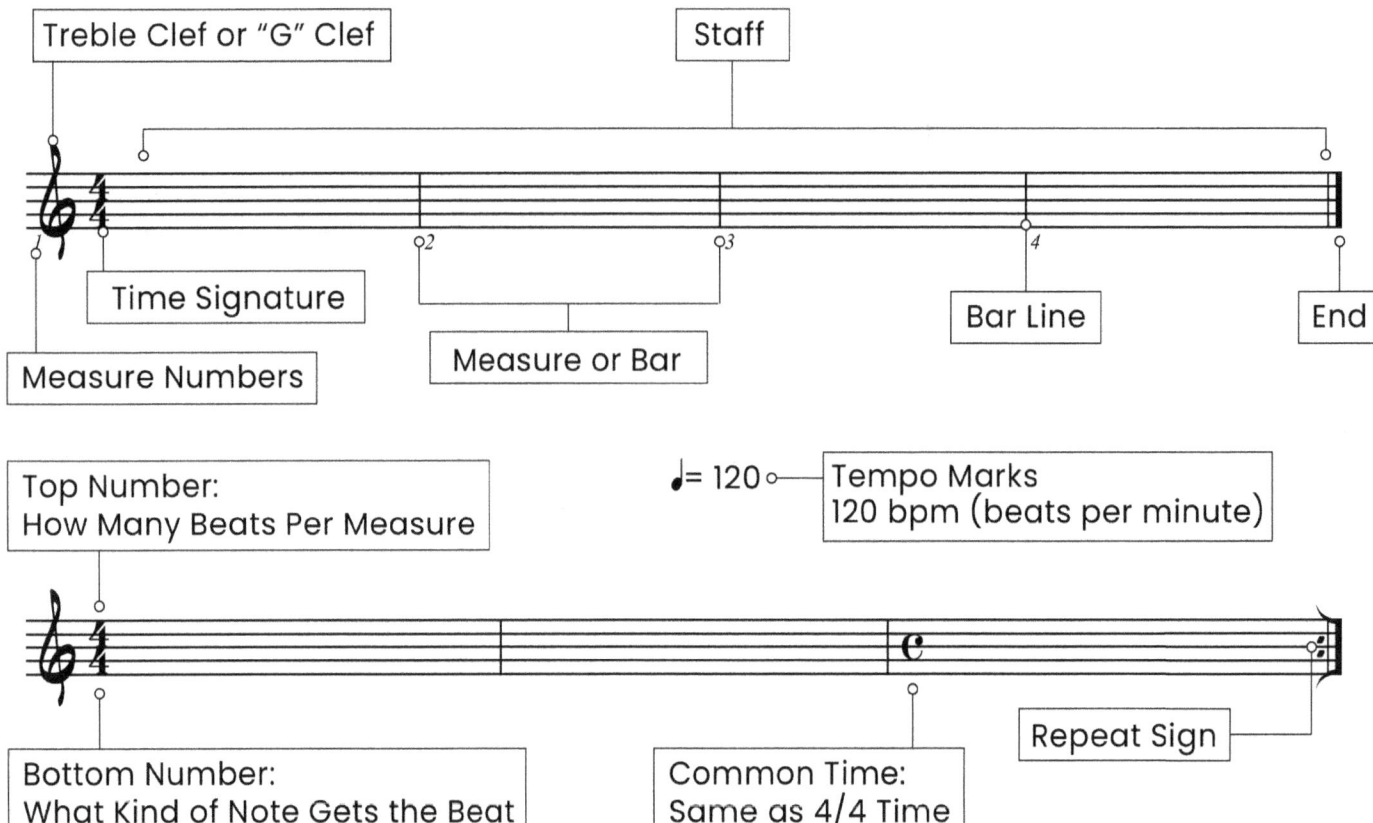

Notes On The Staff: There are seven notes in music (A, B, C, D, E, F, G) and they move up and down alphabetically on the staff.

G A B C D E F G A B C D E F G A B C D E F

How To Remember The Notes:

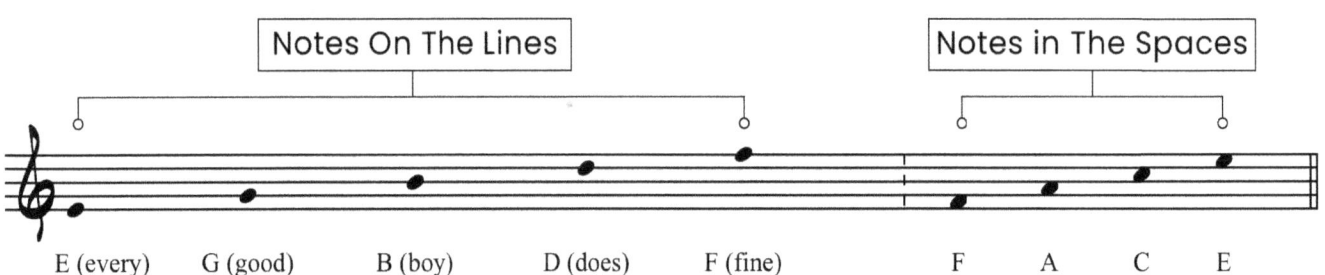

E (every)   G (good)   B (boy)   D (does)   F (fine)   F   A   C   E

A

How To Read TAB

Tablature (TAB) is a form of music reading for the baritone ukulele that uses a 4 line staff and numbers. Each line of the staff represents a string on the baritone and the numbers represent which fret you play on. When looking at the TAB staff it reads like it's upside down on the paper compared to the strings of your baritone. On the TAB staff, the highest line (closest to the sky) represents the 1st string (E string) of the baritone, while the lowest line (closest to the ground) represents the 4th string (D string) of the baritone. When you see 2 or more notes stacked on top of each other on the TAB staff, that means you play those notes at the same time, like a chord.

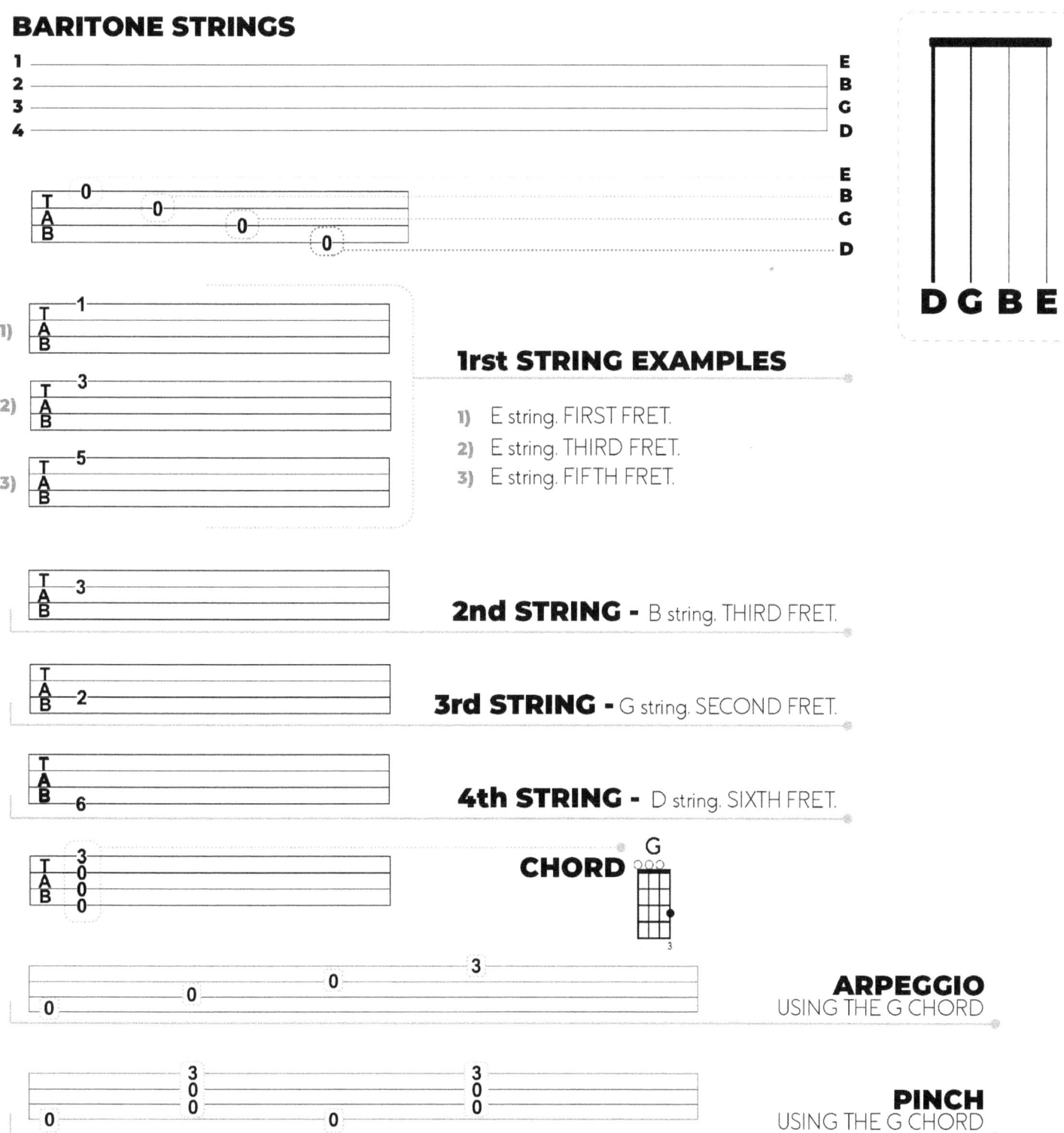

Notes On The Baritone Ukulele Neck

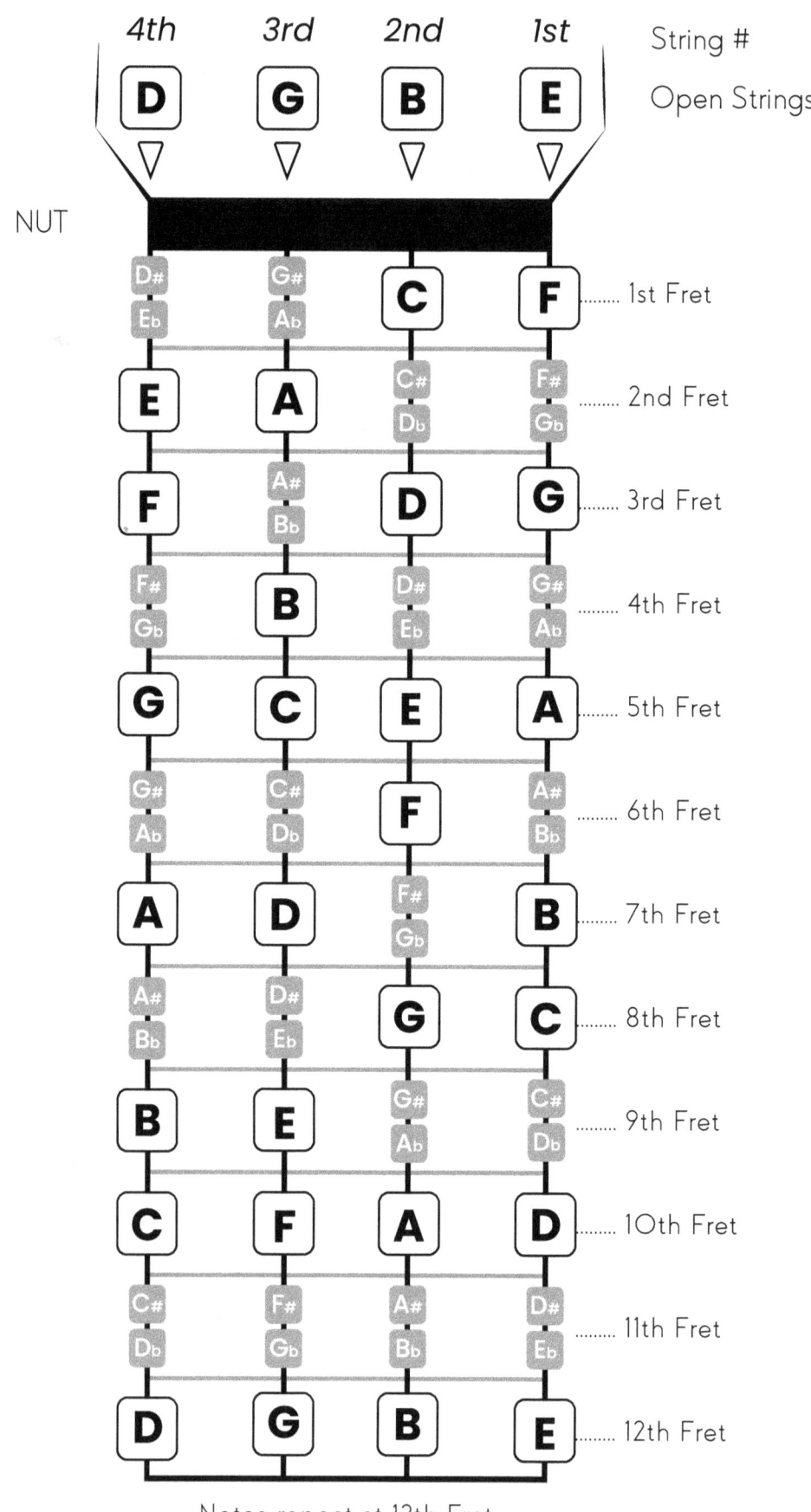

Baritone Ukulele Hands

When playing fingerstyle on your baritone ukulele, you will see both letters and numbers to indicate which fingers to use both for your picking hand and your fretting hand. These letters and numbers will show up in the music notation, TAB, and/or chord diagrams.

FRETTING HAND	PICKING HAND
The left hand for right-handed players, will be indicated in the music or chord diagrams by numbers:	The right hand for right-handed players, will be indicated in the music by letters:
1=Index finger **3**=Ring finger **2**=Middle finger **4**=Pinky finger	**p**=Thumb **m**=Middle **i**=Index **a**=Ring **c**=pinky (not used in this course)

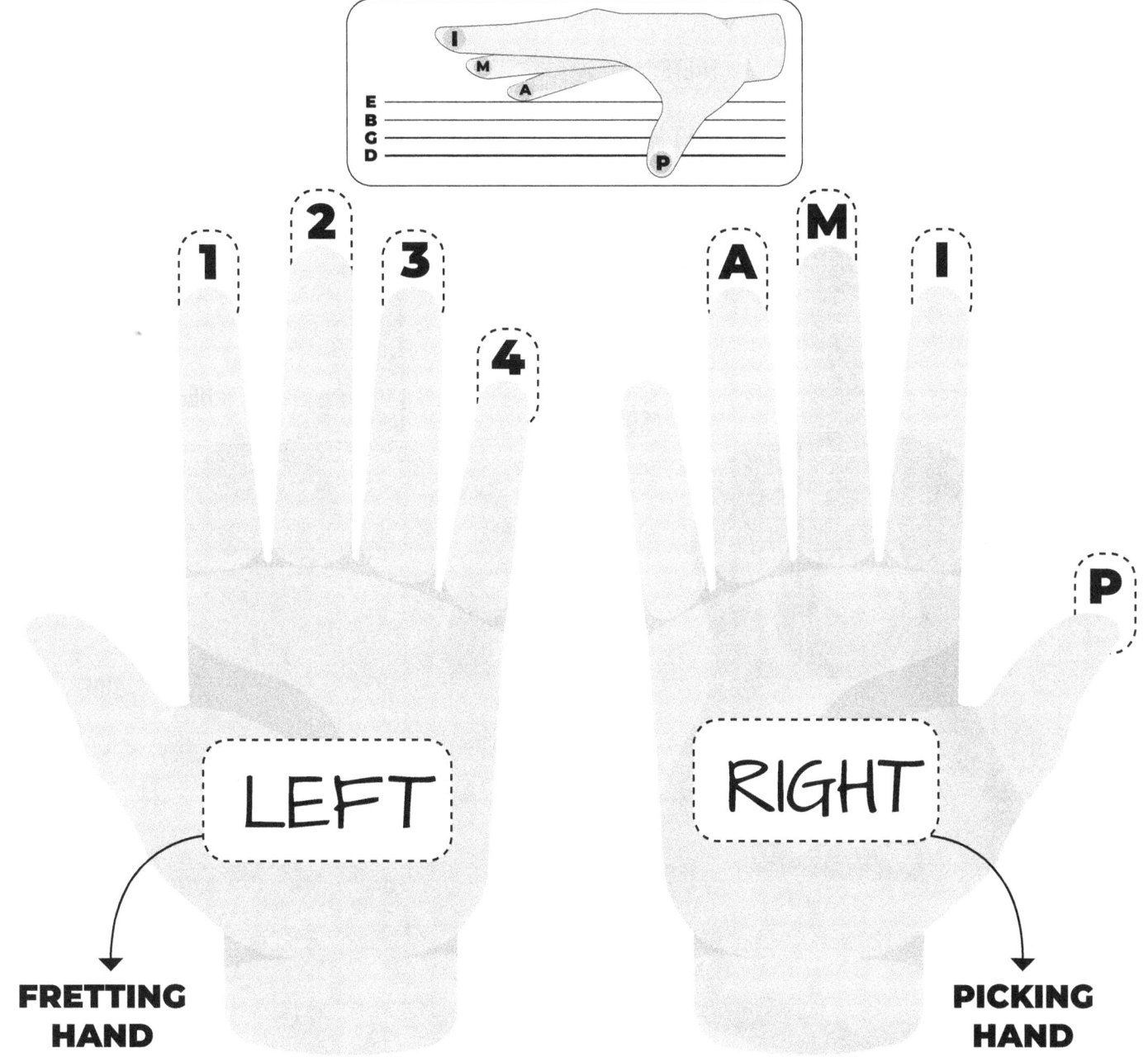

FRETTING HAND

PICKING HAND

Baritone Ukulele Parts

Understanding Chord Diagrams

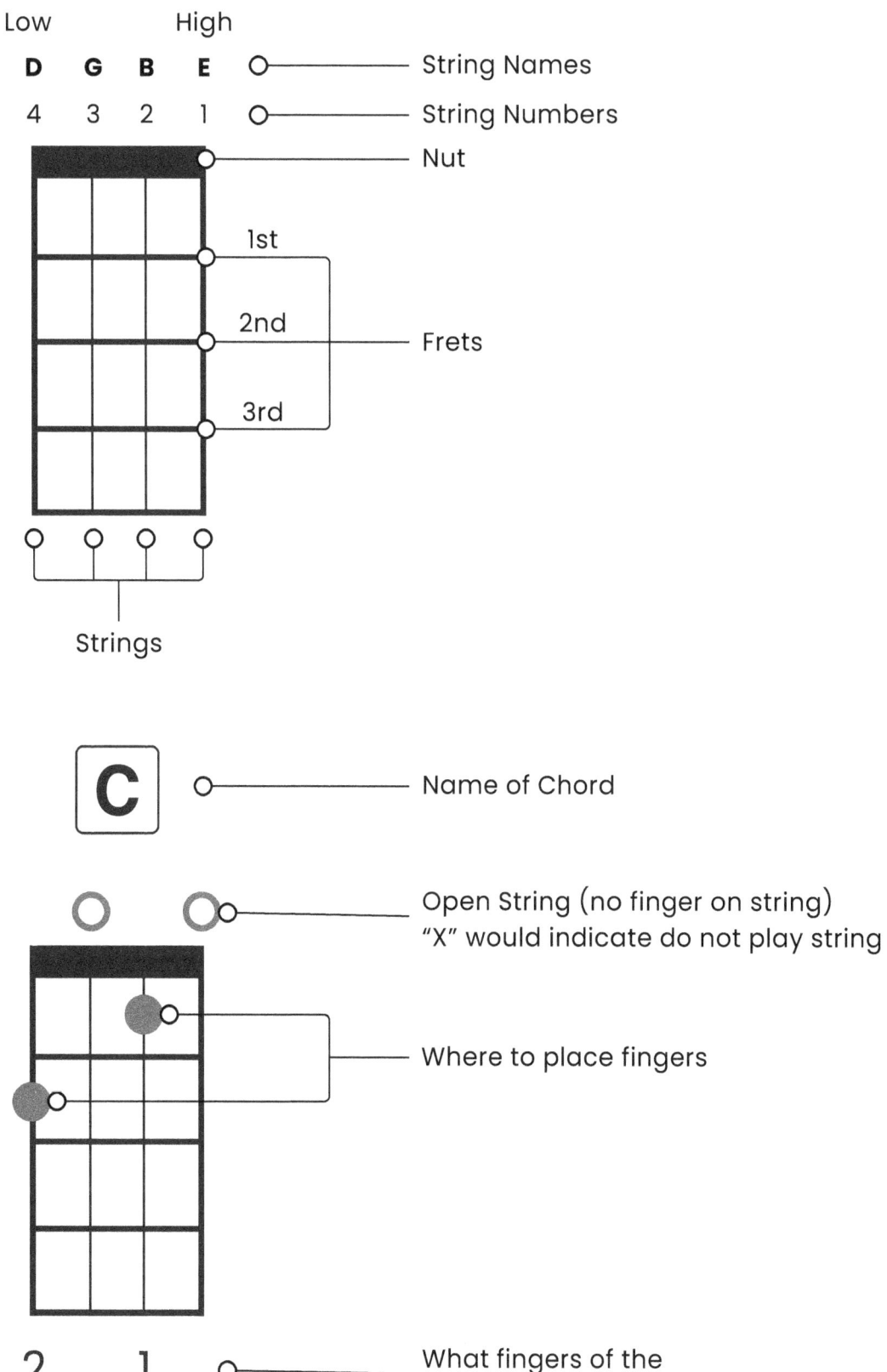

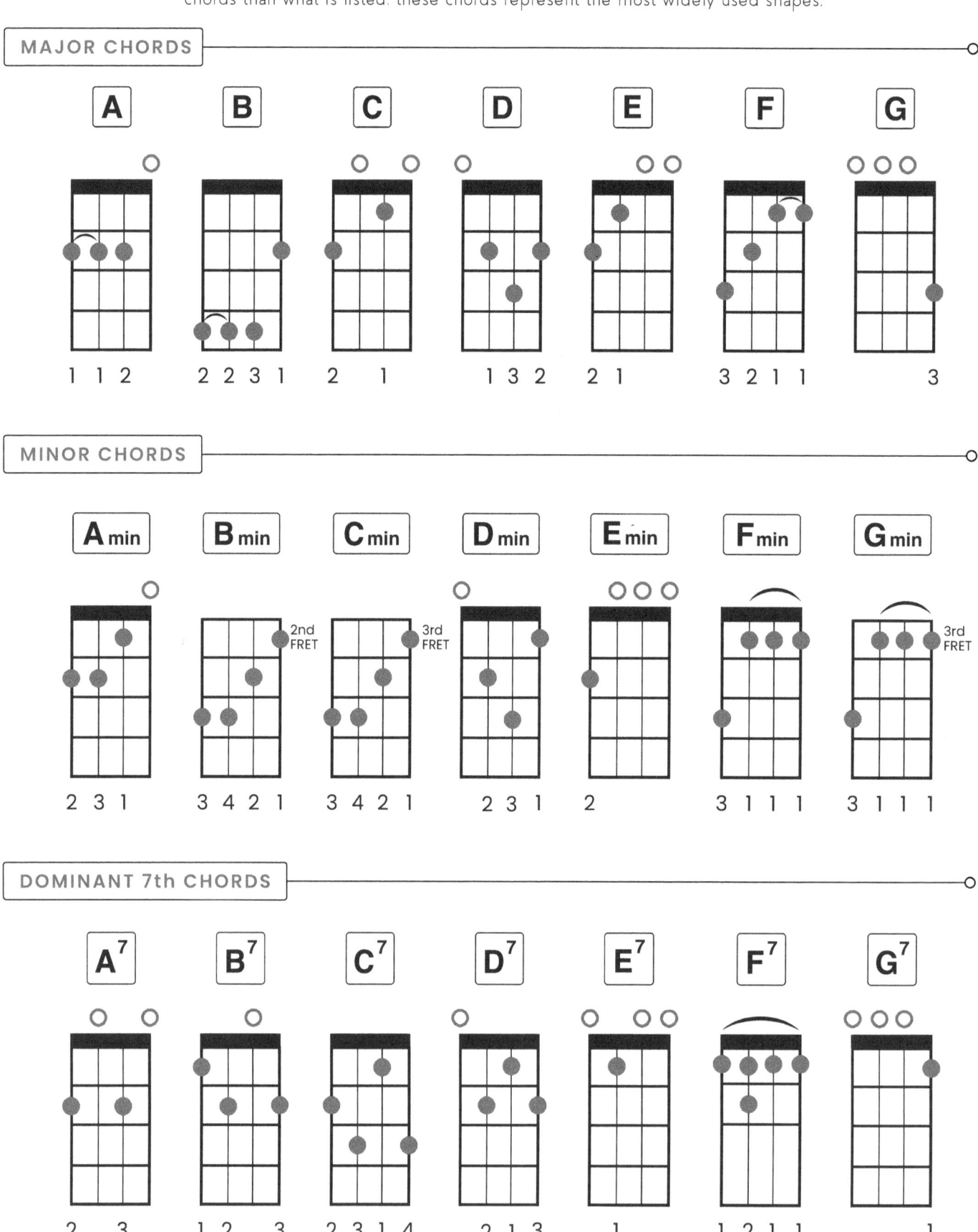

MAJOR 7th CHORDS

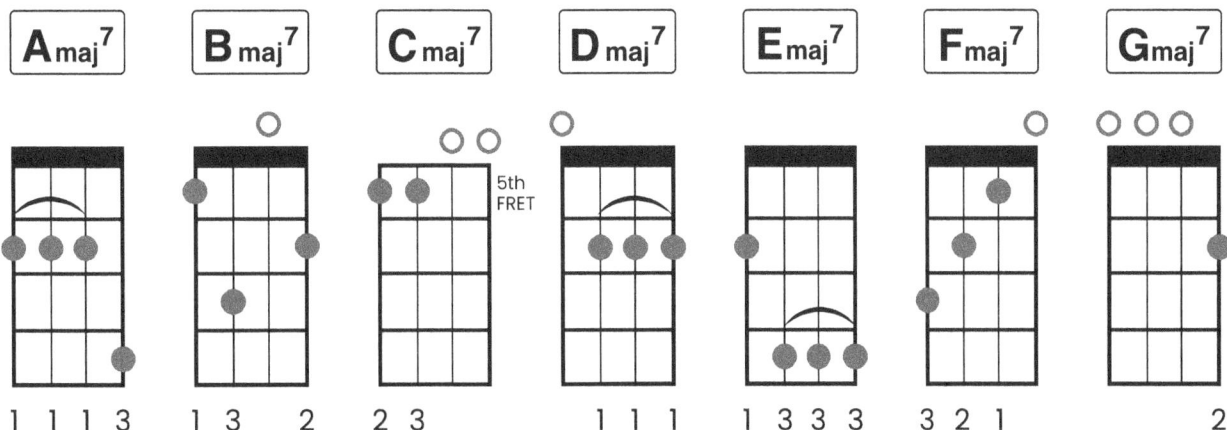

MINOR 7th CHORDS

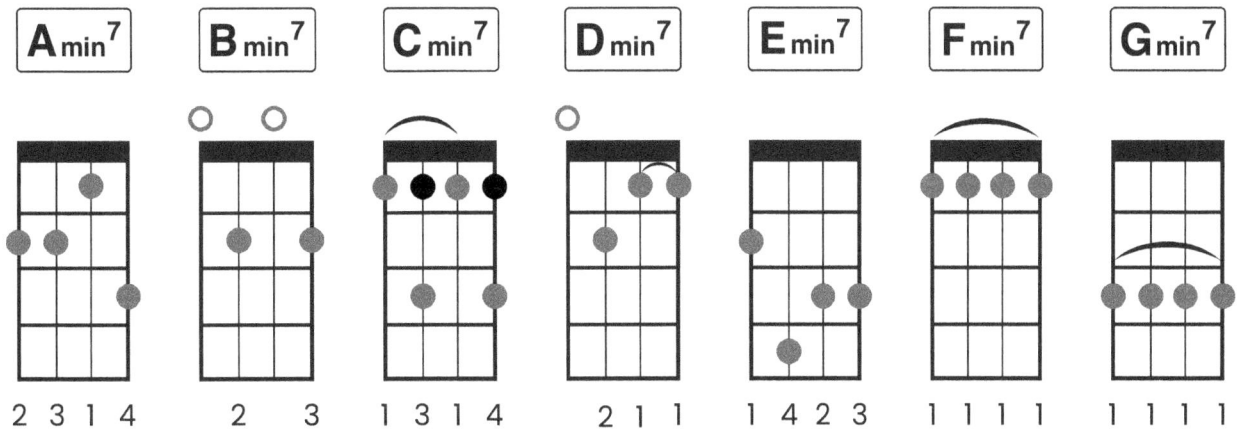

SUS + ADD CHORDS

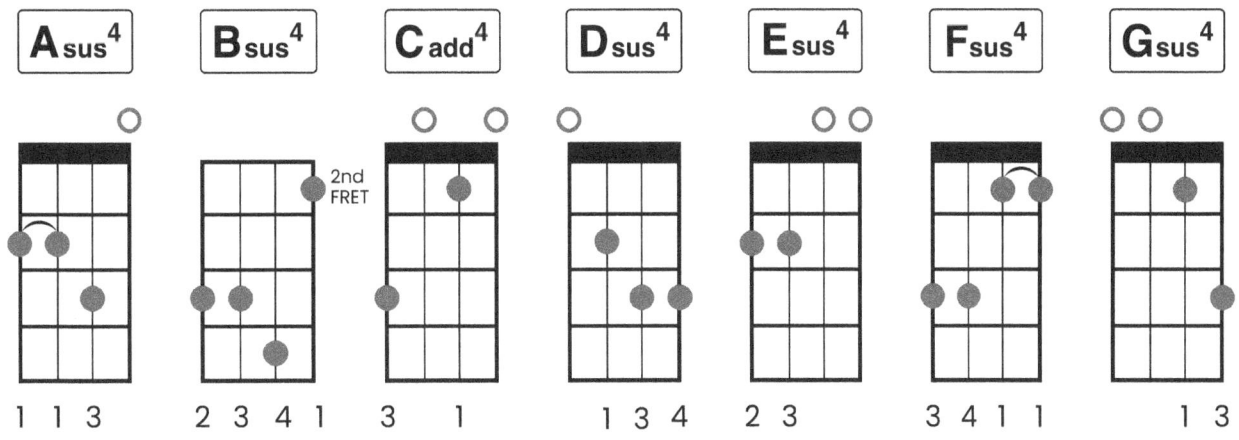

Music Symbols To Know

A variety of symbols, articulations, repeats, hammer on's, pull off's, bends, and slides.

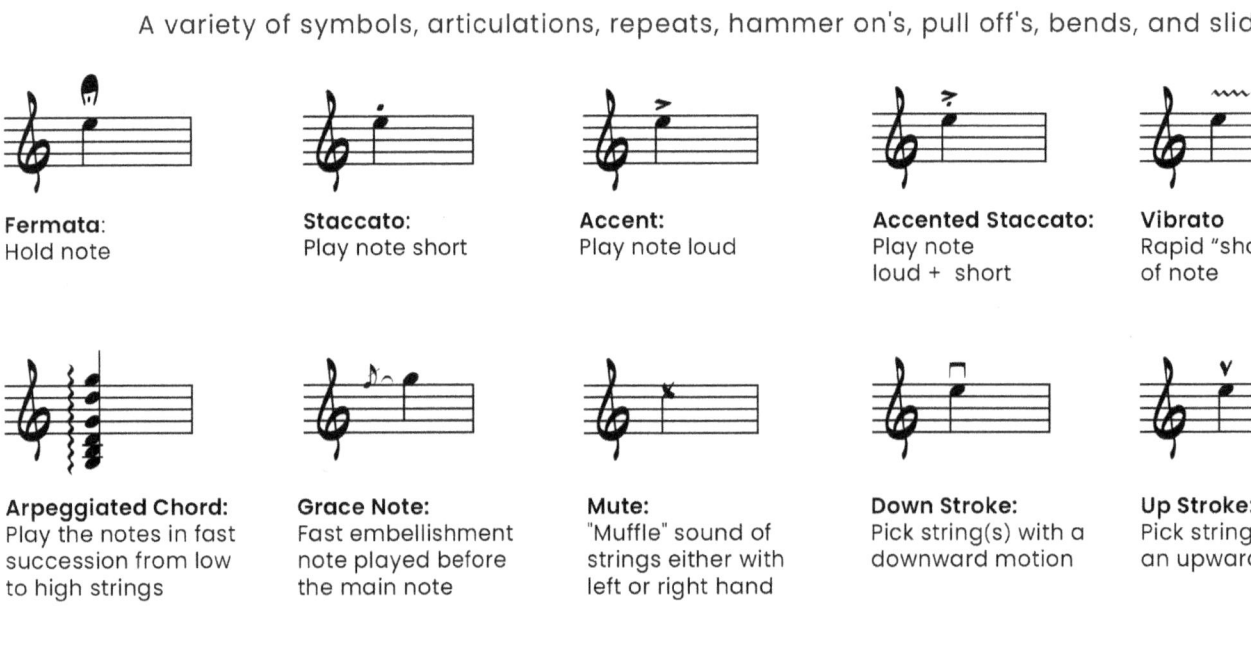

Fermata: Hold note

Staccato: Play note short

Accent: Play note loud

Accented Staccato: Play note loud + short

Vibrato: Rapid "shaking" of note

Arpeggiated Chord: Play the notes in fast succession from low to high strings

Grace Note: Fast embellishment note played before the main note

Mute: "Muffle" sound of strings either with left or right hand

Down Stroke: Pick string(s) with a downward motion

Up Stroke: Pick string(s) with an upward motion

Tie: Play first note but do not play second note that it is tied to

Ledger Lines: Extend the staff higher or lower.

Slash Notation: Repeat notes & rhythms from previous measure

1 Bar Repeat: Repeat notes & rhythms from previous measure

2 Bar Repeat: Repeat notes & rhythms from previous 2 measures

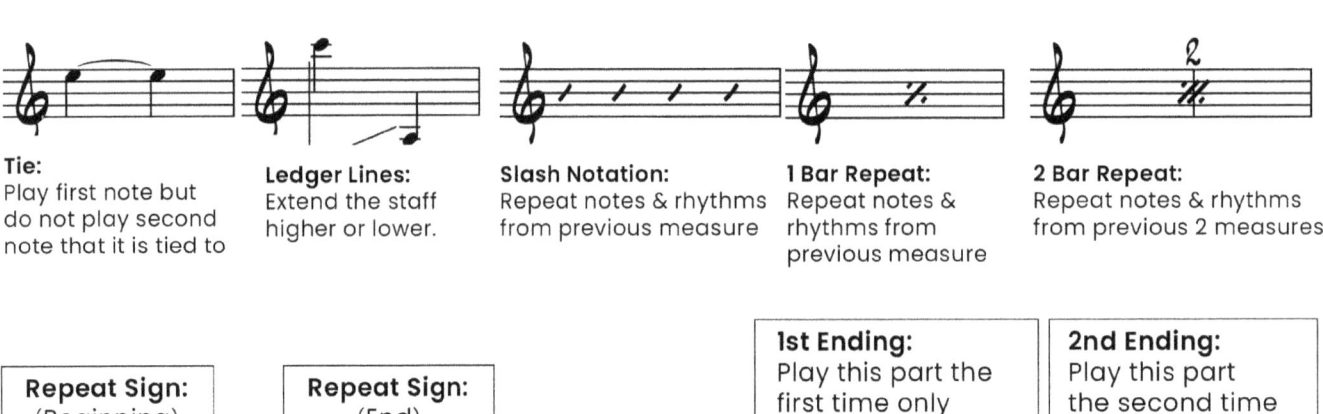

Repeat Sign: (Beginning)

Repeat Sign: (End)

1st Ending: Play this part the first time only

2nd Ending: Play this part the second time

(D.C. AL FINE) — *D.C.* (da capo) means go to the beginning of the tune and stop when you get to *Fine*

(D.C. AL CODA) — *D.C.* means go to the beginning of the tune and jump to *Coda* ⊕ when you see the sign ⊕

(D.S. AL FINE) — *D.S.* (dal segno) means go to the *Sign* 𝄋 and stop when you get to *Fine*

(D.S. AL CODA) — *D.S.* means go to the *Sign* 𝄋 And Jump to the *Coda* ⊕ when you see ⊕

SIM... — Play the same rhythm, strum pattern, or picking pattern as the previous measure

ETC... — Continue the same rhythm, strum pattern, or picking pattern as the previous measure

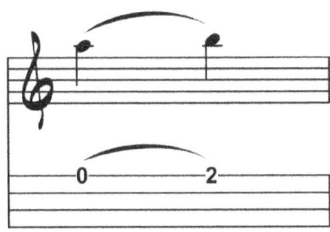

Hammer On:
Pick first note then hammer on to the next note without picking it.

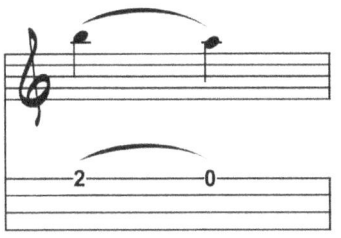

Pull Off:
Pick first note then pull off to the next note without picking it.

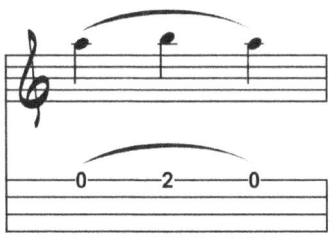

Hammer On & Pull Off:
Pick first note, hammer on to the next note, and pull off to the last note all in one motion.

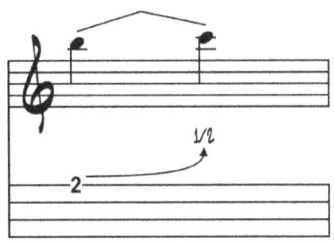

1/2 Step Bend:
Bend the first note a 1/2 step or 1 fret.

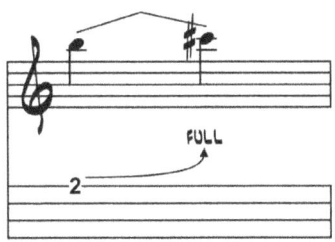

Whole Step Bend:
Bend the first note a whole step or 2 frets.

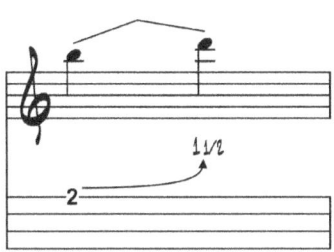

Step & 1/2 Bend:
Bend the first note 1 1/2 steps or 3 frets.

Forward Slide:
Pick first note and slide up to higher note.

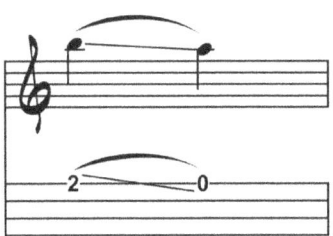

Backward Slide:
Pick first note and slide back to lower note.

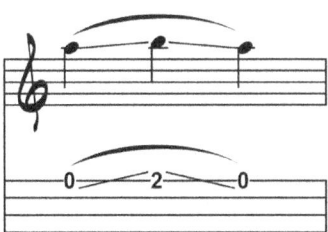

Forward/Backward Slide:
Pick first note, slide up to next note and then slide back.

Slide Into Note:
Slide from 2-3 frets below note.

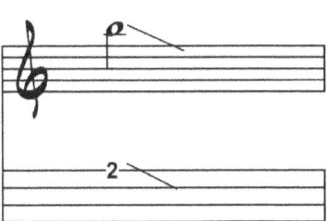

Slide Off Note:
Slide off 2-5 frets after note.

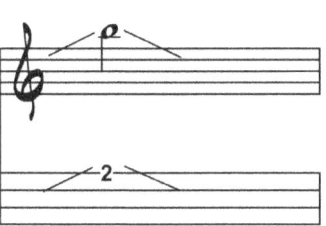

Slide Into Note then Slide Off Note.

ABOUT THE AUTHOR

Terry Carter is a San Diego-based ukulele player, surfer, songwriter, and creator of ukelikethepros.com, rocklikethepros.com and terrycartermusicstore.com. With over 30 years as a professional musician, educator and Los Angeles studio musician, Terry has worked with greats like Weezer, Josh Groban, Robby Krieger (The Doors), 2-time Grammy winning composer Christopher Tin (Calling All Dawns), Duff McKagan (Guns N' Roses), Grammy winning producer Charles Goodan (Santana/Rolling Stones), and the Los Angeles Philharmonic. Terry has written and produced tracks for commercials (Discount Tire and Puma) and TV shows, including Scorpion (CBS), Pit Bulls & Parolees (Animal Planet), Trippin', Wildboyz, and The Real World (MTV). He has self-published over 25 books for Uke Like The Pros and Rock Like The Pros, filmed over 30 ukulele and guitar online courses, and has millions of views on his social media channels. Terry received a Master of Music in Studio/Jazz Guitar Performance from University of Southern California and a Bachelor of Music from San Diego State University, with an emphasis in Jazz Studies and Music Education. He has taught at the University of Southern California, San Diego State University, Santa Monica College, Miracosta College, and Los Angeles Trade Tech College.

Online Courses

The perfect place to learn how to play Ukulele, Baritone Ukulele, Guitar and Guitarlele.

ULTP Roadmap
WHERE TO START?

1) UKULELE BEGINNER
- A. Beginning Ukulele Starter Course
- B. Beginning Ukulele Bootcamp Course
- C. Ukulele Fundamentals Course
- D. Ukulele Practice & Technique Course
- E. Master the Ukulele 1

2) UKULELE INTERMEDIATE
- A. Master The Ukulele 2
- B. Beginning Music Reading
- C. 23 Ultimate Chord Progressions
- D. Beginning Ukulele Fingerstyle Course

3) UKULELE ADVANCED
- A. Ukulele Blues Mastery Course
- B. Beginning Ukulele Soloing Course
- C. Fingerstyle Mastery Course
- D. Jazz Swing Mastery Course

MORE OPTIONS!

FUNLAND
- A. Beginning Ukulele Kids Course Songbook
- B. 21 Popular Songs for Ukulele
- C. The Best Ukulele Christmas Songs
- D. 10 Classic Rock Licks
- E. Guitar Fundamentals

BARITONE UKULELE
- A. Beginning Baritone Ukulele Bootcamp Course
- B. 6 Weeks Baritone Q&A
- C. Baritone Blues Mastery Course
- D. Beginning Baritone Fingerstyle Course

GUITARLELE
- A. Guitarlele Starter Course
- B. 6 Weeks Guitarlele Q&A
- C. Guitarlele Course for Ukulele and Guitar Players
- D. Guitarlele Blues Mastery Course

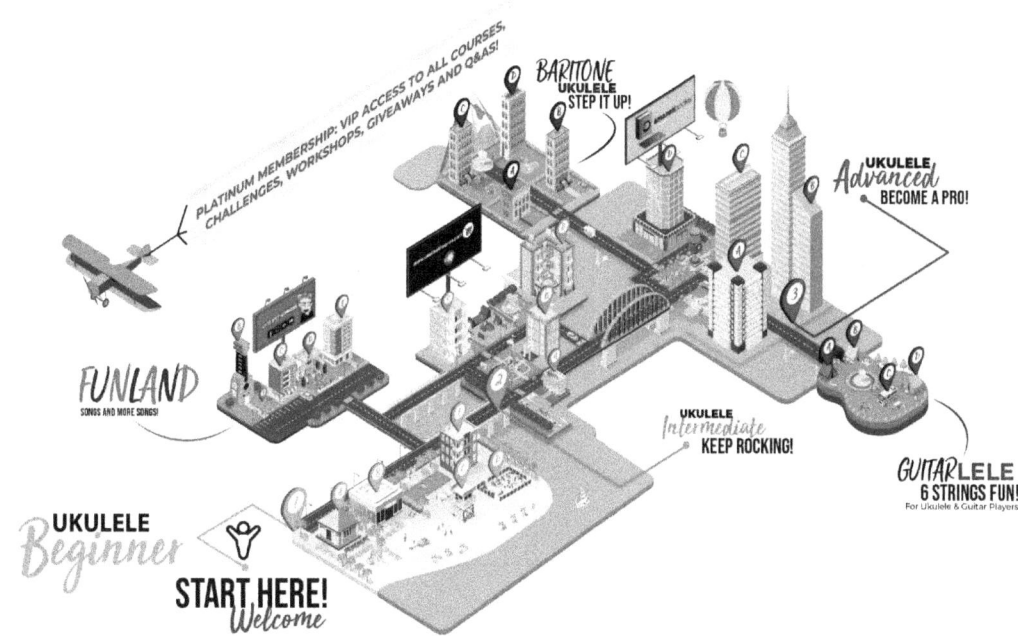

Courses For All Levels
UKELIKETHEPROS.COM

Terry Carter Music Store

All your music needs at the #1 music store, **terrycartermusicstore.com**

Baritones

Ukuleles

Guitars

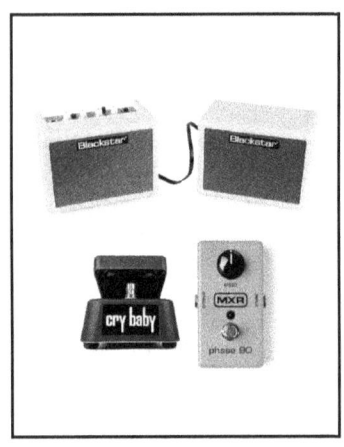

Amplifiers and Pedals

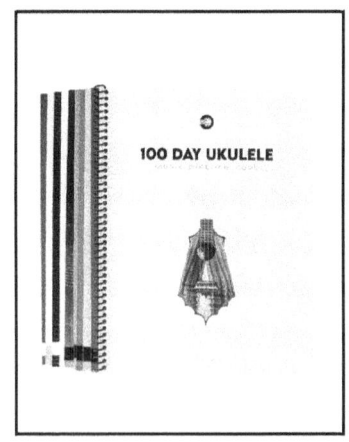

Books

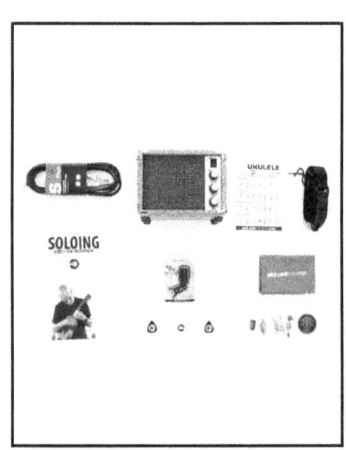

Accessories

UKELIKETHEPROS.COM
BLOG.UKELIKETHEPROS.COM
TERRYCARTERMUSICSTORE.COM
BUYSTRINGSONLINE.COM
VOSTAWORLD.COM

@ukelikethepros

INTERESTED IN GUITAR CONTENT?
ROCKLIKETHEPROS.COM

www.ingramcontent.com/pod-product-compliance
Lightning Source LLC
Chambersburg PA
CBHW051948100426
42738CB00045B/3371